Tool

Training Clinicians to Deliver Evidence-Based Psychotherapy

Development of the Training in Psychotherapy (TIP) Tool

Kimberly A. Hepner, Stephanie Brooks Holliday,
Jessica Sousa, Terri Tanielian

Sponsored by the Bob Woodruff Foundation, Cohen Veterans Network, and the
Robert R. McCormick Foundation

RAND HEALTH CARE

For more information on this publication, visit www.rand.org/t/TL306

Library of Congress Cataloging-in-Publication Data
is available for this publication.
ISBN: 978-1-9774-0142-7

Published by the RAND Corporation, Santa Monica, Calif.

Preface

Ensuring the availability of evidence-based psychotherapy in the community is a critical component of efforts to address rising mental health needs across the United States. To this end, there are many psychotherapy trainings currently designed to increase the competencies of clinicians in community-based settings with respect to delivering evidence-based psychotherapies. However, little is known about the extent to which these trainings incorporate effective approaches for achieving clinical competency in those therapies. This report describes the development of a tool to assess psychotherapy trainings, along with the tool and user guide. The Training in Psychotherapy (TIP) Tool was developed using results from an extensive literature review to identify the core components of trainings that were demonstrably successful in achieving clinician competency in psychotherapy. The literature review was supplemented with consultation with several national experts in psychotherapy training and implementation. The tool was constructed with several potential types of users and uses in mind. The tool may be of interest to organizations that fund psychotherapy trainings, organizations that design and lead these trainings, and organizations and individuals who might be interested in participating in psychotherapy training. This tool is intended to be used by individuals interested in assessing the extent to which a training's approach aligns with evidence- and expert-derived core components for facilitating clinician competency.

This research was funded by the Bob Woodruff Foundation, the Cohen Veterans Network, and the Robert R. McCormick Foundation and carried out within the Access and Delivery Program in RAND Health Care.

RAND Health Care, a division of the RAND Corporation, promotes healthier societies by improving health care systems in the United States and other countries. We do this by providing health care decisionmakers, practitioners, and consumers with actionable, rigorous, objective evidence to support their most complex decisions.

For more information, see www.rand.org/health-care, or contact

RAND Health Care Communications
1776 Main Street
P.O. Box 2138
Santa Monica, CA 90407-2138
(310) 393-0411, ext. 7775
RAND_Health-Care@rand.org

Contents

Figures and Tables

Figures

Tables

Acknowledgments

We are grateful to the experts who agreed to speak with us during the tool development process, including Judith Beck, Katherine Dondanville, Stefanie Losavio, Mark McGovern, Allen Miller, Christine Padesky, Sheila Rauch, David Riggs, Donna Sudak, and Shannon Wiltsey Stirman. Their insights were invaluable and added important context to the evidence from our literature review. Several of these experts also provided targeted feedback on earlier drafts of the Training in Psychotherapy Tool. We appreciate the valuable insights we received from our reviewers, Karen Osilla and Shannon Wiltsey Stirman. We addressed their constructive critiques as part of RAND's rigorous quality assurance process to improve the quality of this document. We also thank Anita Szafran for her contributions to the literature search and Tiffany Hruby for her assistance in the preparation of this document.

Abbreviations

CBT	cognitive behavioral therapy
DoD	U.S. Department of Defense
EBP	evidence-based psychotherapy
GRADE	Grading of Recommendations Assessment, Development, and Evaluation
MDD	major depressive disorder
MeSH	Medical Subject Headings
PILOTS	Published International Literature on Traumatic Stress
PTSD	posttraumatic stress disorder
RCT	randomized controlled trial
SUD	substance use disorder
TIP Tool	Training in Psychotherapy Tool
VA	U.S. Department of Veterans Affairs

CHAPTER ONE

Introduction

Ensuring the availability of evidence-based psychotherapy (EBP) in the community is a critical component of efforts to address the rising mental health needs across the United States. As the research base for the effectiveness of various psychotherapies grows, efforts to ensure that community-based clinicians are aware of the psychotherapies that are recommended for certain mental health conditions have increased. One mechanism for doing so is the development and dissemination of clinical practice guidelines (e.g., American Psychological Association, 2018; American Psychiatric Association, 2018; U.S. Department of Veterans Affairs [VA], 2018). However, publishing these guidelines may not be enough to change clinicians' practice behaviors. The burgeoning psychotherapy implementation and dissemination literature (Karlin et al., 2012; Kettlewell, 2004; McHugh and Barlow, 2010; Schoenwald and Hoagwood, 2001) suggests that additional efforts are often needed to encourage adoption of these recommendations and to facilitate clinician competency with specific techniques, such as training and organizational support. Ensuring the provision of EBPs in community practice settings is essential if individuals are to receive the most-effective available treatments no matter where they get care.

One population that is increasingly seeking mental health care in the community is military veterans. Veterans are a special population of men and women who have served their country, many having faced extraordinary health risks during their deployments. Because many veterans have served on overseas missions, including combat, veterans with service-connected health issues are a clinically complex and potentially vulnerable population. Though VA has increased the number of health professionals working within its facilities and has increased its purchases of care from private-sector providers to accommodate veterans whose needs cannot be met in house, many veterans seek care outside VA. Most veterans enrolled in VA health care have other sources of health coverage, such as TRICARE or employer-sponsored insurance. A study of veterans' overall use of health care found that veterans enrolled in VA health care received only 30 percent of their care from VA, on average (Eibner et al., 2015). In addition, recent changes to how VA purchases care in the community setting has increased the number of veterans eligible for private-sector care. Thus, providers working in the civilian sector are an increasingly important part of the overall health workforce addressing veterans' mental health needs. Some of the most prevalent mental health conditions among veterans are posttraumatic stress disorder (PTSD), major depressive disorder (MDD), and substance use disorder (SUD) (Tanielian, Jaycox, et al., 2008)—conditions for which there are well-established psychotherapies (such as cognitive behavioral therapy [CBT], cognitive processing therapy, and prolonged exposure therapy).

Despite the strong evidence base for certain psychotherapies, evidence-based treatments are not consistently implemented in community-based settings. For example, a 2014 study found that only about one-third (35 percent) of community-based psychotherapists reported that they had been trained and received supervision to deliver at least one EBP for PTSD and at least one for depression (Tanielian, Farris, et al., 2014). Further, only about 30 percent reported that they often or always used techniques associated with at least one of the EBPs for PTSD and major depression (Tanielian, Farris, et al., 2014). These findings suggest that there is indeed a need for increased efforts to equip the community-based mental health workforce to deliver evidence-based treatments.

There are a number of potential barriers to implementing evidence-based practices in community-based settings. These include clinician attitudes, organizational factors (e.g., leadership support), and differences between the settings in which treatments were developed and those in which they are expected to be implemented (e.g., with respect to resources, time, and complexity of the patient population) (Addis, Wade, and Hatgis, 1999; Drake et al., 2001; Schoenwald and Hoagwood, 2001; Southam-Gerow, Hourigan, and Allin, 2009). However, one of the most commonly cited factors contributing to the research–practice gap is the need for effective clinician training (Chambless, 1999; Generali, Foss-Kelly, and McNamara, 2011). In fact, it has been suggested that "perhaps the greatest challenge to [dissemination and implementation] efforts . . . is training clinicians to competently administer treatments" (McHugh and Barlow, 2010).

To address the need for expanded clinician training, efforts to train mental health providers in community settings to implement EBPs have increased. At present, there are dozens of psychotherapy trainings with offerings for community-based mental health care professionals on various psychotherapy approaches. Because these trainings have been designed and implemented across multiple organizations, many psychotherapy training models and approaches that vary in mode and intensity exist (e.g., from short one-session webinars to in-person, multiple-day trainings). Little is known, however, about the extent to which these approaches incorporate proven strategies not only for enhancing clinician knowledge of EBPs (such as CBT for depression) but also for changing clinician behavior to implement such strategies in their clinical settings.

The objective of this report is to describe the development of the Training in Psychotherapy (TIP) Tool, an assessment tool that can be applied to community-based psychotherapy trainings to examine the extent to which their features align with core elements that would enhance the effectiveness of training initiatives. Chapter Two describes the methods used to construct the tool, including the scope and results of our review of the extant literature and discussions with training experts. Chapter Three includes a user guide for the tool with specific instructions and guidance on how to apply the tool to specific psychotherapy trainings. Chapter Four outlines a series of next steps to further refine and validate the tool. Appendixes A and B provide information on the development of the tool and the search terms used to identify relevant literature for review. Appendix C contains the tool itself.

CHAPTER TWO

Identifying Core Elements of Effective Psychotherapy Training

To support the development of the TIP Tool, we employed a two-step process:

1. We conducted a comprehensive literature search to identify the core elements of effective psychotherapy trainings.
2. We conducted a series of key informant discussions with experts on psychotherapy training and implementation science.

Our objectives were to identify the components of psychotherapy trainings that were most critical to clinicians achieving adherence and competence with the particular intervention protocol (Perepletchikova and Kazdin, 2005) and to seek feedback on an early draft of the tool.

Methods

Step 1: Literature Review

Literature Review Overview

We conducted a literature review to identify common elements of psychotherapy trainings and to determine which elements of trainings were shown to be associated with positive outcomes. We conducted a broad search to ensure that we captured a range of trainings in our search, but we limited the results to selected target diagnoses—PTSD, MDD, and SUD. These diagnoses are common for patients who receive psychotherapy in community-based settings, particularly veterans (Tanielian, Jaycox, et al., 2008; Tanielian, Batka, and Meredith, 2017). These are also diagnoses for which there are effective psychotherapies. The search focused on articles that described psychotherapy trainings that trained community-based clinicians to deliver specific EBPs for PTSD, MDD, and SUD that are recommended by the following guidelines:

- VA and the U.S. Department of Defense (DoD) clinical practice guidelines for the management of MDD, PTSD, or SUD (Management of Major Depressive Disorder Working Group, 2016; Management of Posttraumatic Stress Disorder Work Group, 2017; Management of Substance Use Disorders Work Group, 2015)
- American Psychological Association Clinical Practice Guideline for the Treatment of PTSD (American Psychological Association, 2017).

We constructed a search strategy specific to each diagnosis that included the specific recommended EBP (e.g., cognitive processing therapy) and terms related to the target diagnosis, training, evaluation, and outcomes. The scope, article review and data abstraction processes, and summary quantitative results of the literature search are included in Appendix A. The complete list of included psychotherapies appears in Table A.1 in Appendix A, and the search statements appear in Appendix B.

When reviewing the results of the literature search, we focused on articles with descriptions and evaluations of trainings, including community-based trainings and trainings offered within the context of treatment trials (e.g., training provided to study clinicians). Of the 1,845 unique records (e.g., articles, book chapters) identified through database searches and other sources, 113 relevant peer-reviewed articles were abstracted for full-text analysis (see Figure A.1 in Appendix A for a flow diagram that details how the 1,845 records were reduced to the final 113 articles). These 113 articles reported findings on 137 trainings for a range of psychotherapies. We abstracted data on characteristics of trainings, including diagnosis and treatment of focus, timing and level of interactivity, and consultation/supervision format and session review. Most articles presented some type of evaluation data (93 percent of trainings), although the methodology varied substantially, with articles reporting on such outcomes as knowledge, self-efficacy, treatment fidelity, and even patient outcomes.

Focus on Treatment Fidelity

After reviewing the literature, we decided to focus on studies that reported data on treatment fidelity (also called treatment integrity) following a training. We focused on articles reporting on fidelity because these measures can assess whether a training was successful in increasing particular therapeutic skills among clinicians. *Treatment fidelity* is the extent to which a psychotherapy is implemented according to the treatment protocol with good judgment and skill. Fidelity includes both adherence and competence—*adherence* is the extent to which the skills and procedures described in a treatment manual are implemented, and *competence* is the degree to which a clinician implements the treatment procedures with good clinical judgment and skill (Perepletchikova and Kazdin, 2005). Though many articles reported outcomes that assessed the impact that the training had on clinician knowledge or skill, these outcomes do not always translate to improved adherence or competence in clinical practice. In particular, we were interested in articles that reported on whether clinician trainees achieved adherence or competence following the training, preferably with measurements before and after the training.

There are many ways to assess fidelity. The most rigorous involve session review in which audiotaped, videotaped, or live therapy sessions are rated for adherence and competence by an independent rater using a structured coding tool. Fidelity coding can be a resource-intensive process and was not included in all identified articles. We evaluated the method of assessing adherence and competence when available and included the studies that were less rigorous in their assessment of adherence or competence (e.g., articles reporting on trainings that utilized informal assessments of adherence or competence).

Fifty-seven studies included some assessment of fidelity (see Figure A.3 in Appendix A). There was wide variability in how fidelity was operationally defined and assessed. Some studies distinguished between adherence and competence; others did not. Some made reference to "fidelity" or "integrity" without clarifying whether they were referring to adherence, competence, or both. Many articles also reported only on change in adherence or competence from baseline to end point, without stating explicitly whether the trainees reached a minimum or satisfactory level of adherence or competence. We focused on the studies that reported whether clinicians achieved some criterion level of adherence or competence, but we did not exclude studies that reported only on an end-point level of adherence or competence.

Despite this variation in assessment and reporting of fidelity, there were some similarities in fidelity assessment across the more methodologically rigorous articles (i.e., randomized controlled trials [RCTs] of training approaches or treatment RCTs with detailed training protocols). Some of the most commonly reported fidelity assessment tools were the Cognitive Therapy Rating Scale, the Collaborative Study Psychotherapy Rating Scale, the Yale Adherence and Competence Scale, adaptations of or variations on these three scales, and specifically designed scales that were developed for the particular training or training study. Fidelity assessments were completed by clinicians (self-assessment), supervisors, and trained independent observers and coders.

Step 2: Key Informant Input

As we distilled findings from the literature review, we also integrated findings from consultation with five experts. These individuals were selected based on their publication track records and national recognition as experts in the development of and training in specific psychotherapies, psychotherapy training, and implementation science. Four telephone discussions with five experts provided information about best practices in psychotherapy training, as well as important context for the development and potential uses of the TIP Tool. Discussion topics included a description of the psychotherapy training (with such details as format, length, frequency, level of interactivity, trainer-to-trainee ratio, trainer qualifications, the types of content considered essential, consultation/supervision, competency evaluation, and certification), core elements of training, and approaches to training evaluation. We also sought feedback from seven experts on early drafts of the TIP Tool to ensure that items were written clearly, provided sufficient scoring guidance, and adequately reflected the core elements of effective psychotherapy trainings. Selected experts participated in both voluntary activities.

Core Effective Training Elements

In this section, we describe the training elements that our literature review and discussion with key informants identified as important for producing adherence and competence among clinicians. As described previously, when identifying these elements in the literature, we focused on articles reporting an assessment of fidelity: adherence, competence, or both. In most cases, the input from the key informants overlapped with the insights gleaned from the literature review. In a few cases, the input helped to clarify and provide practical examples of each element. The elements that were more commonly reported among successful trainings informed the development of the tool.

Didactic Training Format

There are different types of approaches to training clinicians in an EBP. Psychotherapy training is generally divided into (1) didactic training, which is teaching that describes and demonstrates the therapy, and (2) consultation/supervision, which is applied learning that occurs in treatment settings in which clinicians are actively practicing a psychotherapy or a related skill with clients and receiving feedback from a more experienced clinician on potential ways to improve (Fairburn and Cooper, 2011). Both didactic training and consultation/supervision are typically considered necessary components of learning any new EBP. In this section, we review aspects of didactic training and identify which aspects appear to be associated with effective psychotherapy training.

Didactic Training Timing and Length

Didactic training typically involves an introduction to the psychotherapy and more in-depth training on theory and practice. It generally involves information being delivered through a lecture-style format or web-based program, though this learning may take place through other formats, such as independent study of a training protocol or manual. Didactic training can vary widely in its timing (it can be "massed," in which training is delivered on consecutive days, or it can be spaced out over time), number of sessions, session length, class size, interactivity level, and training content. There does not appear to be any consistent finding in the literature as to the importance of many of these factors, including the format, length, and number of sessions. In general, the trainings that demonstrated clinician adherence or competence in this literature had didactic training that was structured as a two-day workshop or training seminar (e.g., Hunter et al., 2012; Lloyd et al., 2015; Lu et al., 2012). However, there was a wide range of other training formats, lengths, and frequencies.

In our literature review, trainings were offered in a variety of formats, including massed (i.e., one time, consecutive days), spaced out over time, and flexible (leaving the choice of timing to the training participant). In some cases, the format was not specified. Both massed (e.g., Gibbons et al., 2010; Martino et al., 2009; Rawson et al., 2013) and spaced (Fals-Stewart and Birchler, 2002; Miller et al., 2005; Puspitasari, Kanter, Murphy, et al., 2013) trainings demonstrated success in achieving adherence among clinicians who participated. Very few studies directly compared web-based, teleconference, and in-person training formats (Sholomskas, Syracuse-Siewert, et al., 2005), and these studies often varied other aspects of training (e.g., presence or absence of supervision), making it difficult to form conclusions about the relative importance of modality of delivery (Rawson et al., 2013; Sholomskas, Syracuse-Siewert, et al., 2005). The ratio of trainer to trainee (which varied widely) was not evaluated sufficiently to assess whether it was related to the success of the training. Similarly, the experience of trainers was sometimes mentioned descriptively in the literature, but the effect of trainer experience was not generally tested—and, in most cases, the trainer was someone considered an expert or with many years of experience in the given psychotherapy.

Interactivity

Trainings that demonstrate the application of a psychotherapy technique or strategy or that use interactive methods to engage trainees appear more likely to have participating clinicians achieve adherence or competence (e.g., Hepner et al., 2011; Lu et al., 2012; Papas et al., 2010). For example, trainings sometimes used live or video demonstrations of clinical skills. Trainings in the literature used various interactive methods, such as skill practice (e.g., Karlin et al., 2012; Simons et al., 2010), role plays (e.g., Lu et al., 2012), interactive group discussion (e.g., Brooks et al., 2013; James et al., 2001; Shemesh et al., 2011), and feedback on homework assignments (e.g., Puspitasari, Kanter, Busch, et al., 2017). In web- and computer-based trainings, interactive training methods included questions, exercises, and homework assignments asking trainees to apply newly learned material; audio and video case vignettes with clinical skill practice; and case-based simulations.

Interactive exercises, group discussion, and demonstrations have been associated with clinician adherence (Hepner et al., 2011; Morgenstern et al., 2001). One study found that clinicians who completed an interactive computer program demonstrated significantly higher adherence scores on 12-step facilitation for SUD than clinicians who trained with a manual only and no interactive elements (Sholomskas and Carroll, 2006). There is less evidence that interactive components are critical to achieving an increase in clinician competence in a psychotherapy after training, but several findings do support the idea that interactivity increases the likelihood of trainee competence. One study found that competence was higher among trainees taught with interactive learning strategies (skill modeling, skill rehearsal, and group discussion with trainer) than in a self-paced program with less interactivity (Puspitasari, Kanter, Busch, et al., 2017). Another training that utilized role play and practice cases was similarly successful; 91 percent of participating clinicians achieved competence with their first practice case, and the fidelity ratings—a combined measure of both adherence and competence—demonstrated good or excellent fidelity among the clinicians who participated (Lu et al., 2012). Other articles reported improvements in clinician competence with interactive training elements without reporting that clinicians reached a threshold level of competence (Karlin et al., 2012; Lau, Dubord, and Parikh, 2004; Simons et al., 2010).

Trainees appeared less likely to demonstrate adherence and competence in trainings with low interactivity (Puspitasari, Kanter, Murphy, et al., 2013; Weck et al., 2013). In addition to supporting attainment of adherence and competence, trainings with interactive elements (e.g., video demonstrations, role play for skill practice, small- and large-group discussion, and rating other trainees on their treatment fidelity) appear to achieve better outcomes in trainee satisfaction and self-reported self-efficacy (Karlin et al., 2012).

Feedback

Trainings that provided clinicians with feedback during classroom instruction appeared more likely to report successful attainment of adherence and/or competence among clinicians who had completed that training (e.g., Lu et al., 2012; Puspitasari, Kanter, Busch, et al., 2017). There are many ways in which trainings provide trainees with feedback. Examples include comments on clinician homework assignments, group discussion in which clinician case presentations are met with feedback from the trainer (Shemesh et al., 2011), and role-play or skill practice exercises with remarks from the trainer on what went well or what could be improved. Providing trainees with feedback helps to correct misconceptions, clarify areas of confusion, improve understanding or mastery, and guide trainees toward a deeper understanding of the psychotherapy.

According to the literature, many trainings with interactive teaching methods also include feedback. Thus, many of the above-cited examples of interactivity supporting adherence or competence are also examples of the potential importance of feedback. For example, one study examined a trainer-led online program in which trainees engaged in skill rehearsal with feedback from the trainer and other trainees, as well as group discussion and trainer feedback on participant questions about the practical applications of new skills. This training yielded higher trainee competence than a self-paced online training with the same didactic content and less feedback (Puspitasari, Kanter, Busch, et al., 2017). Another training on CBT for SUD reported that 90 percent of clinicians who completed a combination of interactive exercises, discussion, and role play with feedback during classroom learning plus intensive supervision (discussed separately below) received CBT adherence scores that were adequate or better (Morgenstern et al., 2001). Given the overlap between interactive elements and feedback, it is difficult to assess which component might be more critical in supporting trainee adherence or competence.

Integration of Written Materials

Many trainings provide supplemental written materials or handouts to support or supplement didactic training content. Common materials described in the literature include training manuals or guides, tailored handouts developed by the trainer, and books related to the psychotherapy of focus. Materials were shared in hard copy or digital format, and electronic resources were shared either through web-based (e.g., internet portal) or computer-based (e.g., software program) interfaces. Although these materials were generally not tested in the literature for their impact on clinician adherence or competence, they were frequently referenced as a component of didactic training, and it is reasonable to presume that supplemental tools could serve as an implementation support or reference for clinicians after their return to community-based treatment settings. Regarding the use of written materials during trainings, the literature generally did not explicitly address this issue, except in the case of self-guided trainings (e.g., reading a treatment manual), limiting our ability to determine the most effective ways to incorporate written materials during didactic training.

Didactic Training Content

In the literature reviewed, there was often detail provided about the content of the training. For example, it was common for trainings to describe the theory underlying a given psychotherapy, as well as its core techniques (e.g., cognitive restructuring in CBT, imaginal exposure for prolonged exposure). Trainings often covered clinical decisionmaking, and interactive or role-play exercises were often used to give trainees the opportunity to practice these skills. Although studies generally did not test the effectiveness of the specific content of the trainings, it is likely important for any training designed to promote knowledge and skill in a given psychotherapy to touch on these core topics. Theory, core techniques, and clinical decisionmaking were often mentioned as key content areas for trainings during our key informant discussions.

In addition to theory, core techniques, and clinical decisionmaking, there are other topics that are likely important for a training to address, especially in a program designed to promote adherence and competence. One such topic is measurement-based care, which is the systematic administration of symptom measures and use of the information from these measures to inform clinical decisionmaking at the individual patient level (Fortney et al., 2016). Measurement-based care is a component of many EBPs (Scott and Lewis, 2015), in which symptom levels are routinely monitored throughout treatment. In our literature review, training descriptions rarely explicitly mentioned measurement-based care, though it is likely that some trainings reviewed information about how to use patient self-report measures to assess symptom levels and progress during treatment. Because many EBPs do promote regular symptom monitoring, and given increasing evidence that measurement-based care contributes to positive patient outcomes (Fortney et al., 2016), it is likely an important topic to be covered by trainings.

Similarly, a small number of trainings reviewed in the literature touched on the topic of co-occurring disorders. For example, one study focused on training addiction counselors to implement CBT for depression (Hepner et al., 2011). This training explicitly addressed the connections between substance use and mood and provided examples of depression-related thoughts and behaviors that may be common among individuals receiving treatment for substance use disorders. MDD and PTSD are commonly comorbid with SUD among patients receiving care in community-based or VA treatment settings (Brown et al., 2001; Rush et al., 2005; Seal et al., 2011; Watkins et al., 2004). Therefore, addressing co-occurring disorders as part of psychotherapy trainings focused on these diagnoses will ensure that trainees are better prepared to serve the range of patients who present for treatment.

Consultation/Supervision

As stated above, the purpose of consultation or supervision is to provide training on a psychotherapy to clinicians as they are actively applying or practicing that therapy in a clinical setting. Often, *supervision* refers to a situation in which a clinician in training is practicing under the license of the supervising clinician—for example, when the clinician in training is not yet licensed—whereas *consultation* refers to situations in which an independently practicing clinician draws on the expertise of a colleague or other independently practicing clinician for guidance. Under these definitions, supervision is associated with a legal responsibility on the part of the supervisor because the individual being supervised is practicing under his or her license. That said, in reviewing the literature, *consultation* and *supervision* were used mostly interchangeably and, in most cases, referred to situations that were more in line with the definition of *consultation* because the clinicians participating in training were often independent practitioners (though a small number of trainings included clinicians in training as well). Therefore, when we refer to consultation and supervision in the subsequent sections, we are referring largely to consultation arrangements, though many of the findings likely apply to both traditional supervision of unlicensed or retraining clinicians and independent practitioners seeking to strengthen their skills.

By definition, supervision involves the provision of feedback to clinicians about how they are doing with the implementation of a given psychotherapy in practice with actual clients. Supervision can be conducted in groups or individually and can take place in person, over the phone, or via videoconferencing or other technology-enabled methods. Based on the literature, there does not appear to be a defined amount, frequency, or duration of supervision that is deemed necessary or even recommended for most evidence-based practices. Supervision is typically provided after the didactic portion of a training, which gives clinicians the chance to modify or improve their use and understanding of the therapy while they are actively practicing that therapy with clients. Supervision also typically occurs after some form of initial classroom or didactic instruction is completed, although this is not always the case.

Supervision appears to be critical to achieving adherence and competence across target diagnosis and type of psychotherapy. One study found that, after completing CBT training followed by group supervision with audiotaped session review, mean ratings on the Cognitive Therapy Rating Scale reflected moderate adherence and competence, though clinician scores fell below the typically applied threshold for competence (Lopez and Basco, 2015). A recent study of training in cognitive processing therapy for PTSD found that therapists who received group consultation achieved better patient outcomes than those with no consultation (Monson et al., 2018). Another training for interpersonal therapy in the Veterans Health Administration found that, while participating in telephone-based consultation after the conclusion of a three-day training workshop, clinicians increased in competence from baseline to the first patient and then increased again from the first patient to the second patient, suggesting that ongoing practice while receiving consultation can result in continued improvement of skills (Stewart et al., 2014). Similarly, a training for acceptance and commitment therapy for MDD found that trainees significantly increased in competence during the consultation period (Walser et al., 2013).

Although most trainings that offered consultation or supervision did so following completion of the didactic and initial skill practice elements of training, trainings that conducted supervision concurrent with training were also successful in bringing trainees to competence (Lau, Dubord, and Parikh, 2004). However, there is limited support in the literature for conclusions regarding the importance of the timing, frequency, or duration of supervision for supporting clients in achieving adherence and competence. That said, some of the literature reviewed above suggests that a longer supervision period or requiring supervision for a certain number of cases may help to ensure that clinicians have an adequate opportunity to practice skills and ultimately reach adherence and competence.

There is some evidence that the format of consultation/supervision may make a difference. For example, one study found that CBT competence increased over time among clinicians who received group consultation with review and group discussion of audiotaped therapy sessions but that CBT competence decreased over time among some of the clinicians who had received individual consultation with review and one-on-one discussion of audiotaped therapy sessions (Wiltsey Stirman, Pontoski, et al., 2017). However, few studies compared the format of consultation/supervision, and this result was not consistently found across the literature. Literature we reviewed related to specific trainings also provided little detail about the specific content of consultation and what elements may be effective. There is some evidence from the implementation and dissemination literature that suggests that such elements as helping clinicians understand appropriate ways to adapt a psychotherapy for a given patient, ensuring that consultation is tailored to an individual clinician's needs, and incorporating behavioral rehearsal or modeling may improve the effectiveness of consultation/supervision (Bearman et al., 2013; Rosen et al., 2016; Wiltsey Stirman, Gutner, et al., 2016). However, more work is needed to understand what content is most critical for supporting adherence and competence.

Certification

There is little evidence regarding the influence that certification has on the success of a training in bringing trainees to adherence or competence. Certification was not often mentioned in the literature reviewed, and, when it was described, there was great variability in the threshold specified for certification. In some cases, certification was equivalent to a certificate of participation in the training, in that completion of the training was all that was required for providers to be considered certified. In other cases, certification required participation in the training followed by some demonstration of knowledge, skill, or competence. The most restrictive definitions of certification required that trainees submit a specified number of audio-recorded therapy sessions and obtain a passing score on a standardized assessment of adherence or competence. In most cases, however, there was no mention of certification in the articles included in this review.

Although the literature did not reveal an association between certification and clinician adherence/competence, there are challenges to examining that link. For example, many studies focused on the more immediate outcomes of a psychotherapy training. As described, some of the more rigorous certification programs require clinicians to submit case examples, and it may take some time after a training has been completed for a clinician to have a sample case to submit. Another challenge is that certification requirements can vary by psychotherapy type. For example, our key informant feedback highlighted that cognitive processing therapy offers "provider status" but no certification and that there are other psychotherapies for which national certification is not available. Certification is available in CBT (e.g., through the Academy of Cognitive Therapy), but trainings do not necessarily follow clinicians after their completion of training and consultation to determine the number of people who go on to obtain certification.

However, without standard certification criteria, determining when someone has achieved adherence or competence or is ready to practice a given psychotherapy is at the discretion of the individual participant. Certification is a way to emphasize the importance of formally testing a clinician's skills, rather than presuming that completing training has been sufficient to attain adherence and competence. In this way, encouraging trainees to obtain certification may provide an incentive for clinicians to reach those specified thresholds.

Program Evaluation

Evaluation strategies varied widely across this sample, and articles reported on process measures and patient and clinician outcomes. The more rigorous evaluations included pre/post assessments of adherence and competence, while less rigorous assessments included such metrics as process measures (e.g., clinician satisfaction); clinician self-reported self-efficacy, skill, or behavior change; and patient outcomes, including symptom severity and quality of life. Although there is little evidence regarding the importance of the evaluation of trainings in shaping their effectiveness, evaluation data are likely critical to continuing to improve the training.

Implementation Facilitation

Organizational context and implementation-related factors are important to consider when asking clinicians to change their clinical practice, such as delivering a new EBP (Beidas and Kendall, 2010; Wiltsey Stirman, Gutner, et al., 2016). Our literature review did not focus specifically on organizational or implementation factors, so this literature did not address a link between implementation factors and adherence and/or competence. Still, implementation factors were referenced as a consideration in several articles. For example, one qualitative analysis of cognitive processing therapy training in VA residential programs found that facilitators of use of the psychotherapy in clinical practice included implementation support, availability of additional resources, and the championing of implementation by administrators on site in clinical practice settings (Cook et al., 2015). Anticipating the challenges associated with implementation, another training provided troubleshooting support to coach clinicians on implementation challenges during the consultation period (e.g., Miller et al., 2005).

Our key informant discussions suggested the utility of assessing organizational context and potential implementation barriers as part of psychotherapy training. These discussions also highlighted that implementation barriers make it challenging to design and implement trainings. If clinicians have too few patients on their caseloads, they might not have adequate opportunity to practice the psychotherapy, or, if clinicians are too overwhelmed and pressed for time in their settings, they might not feel that implementing the psychotherapy is an option. One training described adapting content and supports to address implementation barriers (e.g., providing web-based resources, providing initial support before training, or connecting clinicians with other clinicians learning to practice the psychotherapy) (Cook et al., 2015). As described here, there is mounting evidence that, no matter how good training is, EBPs may not necessarily be delivered competently over the long term without sufficient awareness of the ways in which organizational factors can influence implementation success and the need for implementation support. Although psychotherapy trainings have not historically addressed these issues, their inclusion may increase the likelihood that clinicians are able to deliver the EBP with fidelity in their settings.

Clinician Characteristics

A number of themes in the literature appeared to be less central to fidelity but still potentially important in terms of the impact on clinician-related training outcomes. Our literature review suggested a relationship between the baseline qualifications, knowledge, beliefs, and experience of clinicians and their likelihood of reaching adherence and competence after the completion of a training. For example, some studies found that master's-level clinicians had higher competence than bachelor's-level clinicians after completion of the same training—a training that was successful in achieving high levels of adherence and competence among both cohorts of trainees (Fals-Stewart and Birchler, 2002; Meier et al., 2015). Studies differed in their findings about the relative importance of general clinical experience and clinical experience with a specific psychotherapy. Several studies found that past clinical experience with a therapy was more important in achieving competence than the overall length of general clinical experience (James et al., 2001; McManus et al., 2012), although other studies found that clinicians with experience in a particular therapy were similarly successful in achieving adherence and competence to those without specific experience in that therapy (Gibbons et al., 2010; McIndoo, 2016). Some articles from the general psychotherapy training literature suggest that theoretical orientation may not be associated with training outcomes (Creed et al., 2016). Regardless, clinicians with less experience and training can still achieve adherence or competence.

It may not be advisable for clinicians with less experience to self-train using a manual, and supervision might be particularly helpful for this population in implementing EBPs (Chu, 2008). One study that reviewed CBT training practices found that there were multiple studies that, in an attempt to maximize opportunity for feedback, provided more training to clinicians who were starting out with less experience (Rakovshik and McManus, 2010). That said, there were some studies that found no effect of a provider's years of clinical experience (Eftekhari et al., 2015; Ekers, Dawson, and Bailey, 2013), so there is a need for more research in this area.

Limitations

There is considerable variability in the way in which fidelity is defined and measured and in the extent to which fidelity is explored or addressed in the psychotherapy training literature. This variation exists across different types of psychotherapy, diagnoses of focus, and trainings, but there is also variation within individual psychotherapies. For example, articles about CBT trainings sometimes distinguish between fidelity to "generic CBT skills" and fidelity to "CBT-specific interventions" (Larson et al., 2013). Similarly, the way in which competence is assessed also varies in the literature, making it difficult to reach conclusions. For example, there is variability in terms of the extent to which clinician competence on a specific therapy (e.g., cognitive processing therapy) is distinguished from general clinician competence in working with clients (Fairburn and Cooper, 2011). Such variations make it difficult to draw conclusions across the literature. In addition, many trainings operationalize outcomes using such outcomes as knowledge tests or skill assessment during role play, but the disadvantage to this is that there is not good evidence to suggest that knowledge translates to behavior change.

Our literature review suggests that competence is harder to achieve than adherence, although this is not necessarily consistent across different psychotherapies. For example, one motivational enhancement therapy training for SUD found that adherence was harder to attain than competence (Martino et al., 2009). Many other studies of training outcomes for CBT, behavioral activation, and other psychotherapies found that competence was more difficult to achieve than adherence (Fals-Stewart and Birchler, 2002; Hepner et al., 2011; Hunter et al., 2012; Puspitasari, Kanter, Busch, et al., 2017; Puspitasari, Kanter, Murphy, et al., 2013; Rawson et al., 2013). The variability in results across psychotherapies presents a challenge for designing a tool with broad applicability; however, future research may help to determine whether the elements needed to reach adherence and/or competence vary across psychotherapies, which would then inform modifications to the tool.

Documentation of the details of psychotherapy training in the literature we reviewed was highly variable in both content and the degree of detail provided about training and supervision, making it difficult to reach overarching conclusions. It was often difficult to know whether something was excluded or was simply not mentioned in the literature. For example, 39 percent of trainings did not provide a description of the didactic or interactive content, and 20 percent of trainings did not mention supervision or consultation. Of those that mentioned consultation/supervision, 26 percent did not specify format. There is a need to better evaluate the format, spacing, duration, and structure of trainings, given how little is established in the literature about the importance of each of these variables to achieving competence and adherence among newly trained clinicians (Chu, 2008).

The homogeneity of the literature in this particular sample also influences our ability to draw conclusions that transcend type of psychotherapy. In the articles we reviewed, 55 percent of the trainings were CBT-focused. There was some consistency in findings across all psychotherapies, but it was difficult to formally explore potential differences without a sizable sample of articles for each of the psychotherapies. It may be that the importance of certain training elements varies by psychotherapy. For example, an approach like behavioral activation may require less-intensive training than a more complex psychotherapy, such as acceptance and commitment therapy (Jacobson, Martell, and Dimidjian, 2001; Rhodes et al., 2014) or CBT. It is also important to note that our review of the literature was limited to psychotherapies with a strong evidence base; therefore, we did not consider the topic of the training (i.e., which psychotherapy was being trained) as a potential domain for the tool. That said, it is an important consideration when developing and selecting trainings.

Lastly, there was great variability in research methodology across the psychotherapy training literature identified by our team. There were only a handful of training RCTs, and quasi-experimental studies on trainings were not common. The majority of the studies that reported outcomes for evaluations of trainings were pre/post or simply descriptive. Another review of clinician training on psychotherapies found that only a small proportion of the studies identified had utilized rigorous study methodologies (Herschell et al., 2010).

Summary

To develop the TIP Tool, we conducted a literature review, which was supplemented by consultation with experts on psychotherapy training and implementation science. This chapter summarized the results of these efforts, with the ultimate goal of identifying the elements of psychotherapy trainings that have been shown to lead to trainee adherence and competence. Aspects of trainings that emerged as relevant included the level of interactivity of the didactic components of trainings and the availability and format of consultation/supervision for trainees. We used the results of this literature review to inform the development the TIP Tool.

CHAPTER THREE

User Guide

The TIP Tool is designed to assess trainings for community-based providers with respect to how they align with the core elements of trainings identified as potentially effective in our review of the literature and discussion with experts. The tool was constructed with several potential users and uses in mind. Regarding users, the tool may be of interest to organizations that fund trainings and organizations that design and lead trainings, as well as organizations and individuals who might be interested in participating in trainings.

In turn, organizations and individuals could use the tool for multiple reasons. First, it could be used to determine whether an existing training has the features necessary to achieve the goal of that training—whether it be to build initial knowledge in a given area, teach basic skills, or help clinicians to achieve adherence and competence in a given psychotherapy. Second, organizations could use the information to determine which features to incorporate when designing a new training. Third, organizations or individuals could use the tool to select among different types of trainings so they can weigh the relative strength of each for producing clinician competency. Fourth, the tool may also be helpful for those organizations interested in improving or enhancing their own training approaches. For example, by reviewing the descriptions of what constitutes each score within a given domain, a program may identify elements that could be incorporated to build its current capacity. Finally, researchers who study clinician psychotherapy training or conduct psychotherapy research may find the tool useful in documenting the details of the training approach that was used. As highlighted in Chapter Two, we identified several gaps in the psychotherapy training literature, and more thorough documentation of training could help to address outstanding questions about core, effective training elements. These potential audiences and uses are summarized in Table 3.1.

This chapter provides specific guidance on how to use the tool. The chapter begins by reviewing general principles for how an organization or individual would select a training to rate and then provides a detailed guide to applying the rating criteria and scoring the measure.

Applying the Tool to Evaluate Trainings

Organizations may offer multiple types of trainings. In this case, there are different ways in which this tool could be applied. One option is to complete the tool based on a *typical training* offered by the organization. Specifically, an organization could select a representative program and apply the tool based on that training. Although the results may not reflect all trainings offered by the organization, they would characterize a typical type of training for that organization. Another option is to score the tool based on the *capabilities* that an organization can

Table 3.1
Potential Users and Uses of the TIP Tool

Potential Users	Ways the Tool May Be Used
Organizations that fund trainings	• Evaluate or compare existing trainings to determine whether they have the features necessary to achieve the stated goals of the training and funder.
Organizations that design or lead trainings	• Evaluate an existing training to determine whether it has the features necessary to achieve the goals of the training. • Determine what features should be incorporated when designing a new training. • Improve or enhance existing training approaches.
Individuals or organizations interested in participating in trainings	• Evaluate an existing training to determine whether it has the features necessary to meet the needs and expectations of the potential trainees. • Select among trainings when multiple options are present.
Researchers who study clinician training or psychotherapy	• Document detailed elements of the training approach used.

offer as part of a training. Though each element might not be present in every training, scoring the tool in this way would provide a sense of the highest capacity the program can offer within each domain. Finally, the tool could be applied individually to *multiple trainings* within an organization. For example, if a training is tailored for a specific audience or organization and has different features from those of a training for another audience or organization, the tool could be completed separately based on each individual program. This would provide a more nuanced perspective on each specific training offered by the organization.

Characterizing Psychotherapy Trainings

Psychotherapy trainings can vary substantially in their scopes and objectives. Some trainings may be designed to provide clinicians with an introduction to a psychotherapy, such as the evidence base, theoretical underpinnings, and core elements. These trainings are valuable in that they may serve as a primer to increase a clinician's familiarity with a given psychotherapy. At the other end of the spectrum, some trainings may be designed to teach clinicians to implement a given psychotherapy in a clinical setting with fidelity. This type of training focuses not only on increasing a clinician's knowledge but also on building specific skills needed to implement the psychotherapy with adherence and competence.

Given this potential variability, this tool was designed to capture the full range of different psychotherapy trainings. In developing the tool, we considered three categories of psychotherapy trainings, described in more depth in Table 3.2. The first type of training is designed to *raise awareness*—that is, build a clinician's familiarity with a given psychotherapy. The second type of training is designed to promote *skill-building*. The third type of training is designed not only to build skills but also ultimately to *support competence.*

Because some trainings may implement techniques across these different categories, we have considered them along a continuum for purposes of constructing our training rating tool. For example, a training that is designed to raise awareness will likely earn a lower overall score than a training that is designed to support competence. In this way, a lower score would not necessarily be interpreted as reflecting a training that performs worse than others; instead, the

Table 3.2
Characterizing Psychotherapy Trainings

Type of Training	Description
Raising Awareness	These trainings are designed to provide an overview or introduction to a psychotherapy. Although specific therapeutic techniques or skills may be discussed, this is largely communicated in an informational or didactic manner.
Skill-Building	These trainings are designed not only to introduce a given psychotherapy but also to provide the foundation for and develop associated skills and therapeutic techniques. These trainings are designed to help promote positive change in clinical practice.
Supporting Competence	These trainings are designed not only to begin developing skills consistent with a given psychotherapy but also to help clinicians achieve adherence and competence—that is, to prepare clinicians to implement a psychotherapy with fidelity after completion of the training.

lower score may indicate that the training is achieving its objective of raising awareness but perhaps does not include the objectives of promoting skills or clinician competence/fidelity. More details about scoring and interpreting the results of the tool are provided below.

Guidance for Using the Tool

The TIP Tool includes two main sections. The first section gathers information about the training and its characteristics. This section focuses on descriptive characteristics, such as the target psychotherapies, target diagnoses, format, and timing of the training. This part of the tool is not scored, as these features were not consistently associated with better outcomes in the literature. Instead, it is designed to provide context and background on the training.

The second section consists of the scored domains of the tool. The section is organized into five domains, based on our review of the literature and consultation with experts in psychotherapy training and implementation/dissemination. These domains are as follows:

- **Didactic training format:** This domain includes features of the didactic portion of a training, including length of training, level of interactivity, and provision of feedback.
- **Didactic training content:** This domain focuses on the topics covered in the didactic portion of the training, such as core techniques and theory and clinical decisionmaking.
- **Consultation/supervision:** This domain focuses on the consultation/supervision component of a training, including the availability of consultation/supervision and characteristics of consultation/supervision (e.g., length, how the review of sessions is conducted).
- **Program evaluation:** This domain is designed to capture any evaluation that is incorporated into the training, including participant satisfaction and assessment of knowledge and skills.
- **Implementation facilitation:** This domain focuses on the incorporation of implementation of the psychotherapy into the trainee's practice and organization into the training.

Scoring the TIP Tool

Each of the items in the tool is rated on a scale from 1 to 5. This scale is anchored to the three categories of trainings described above: A score of 1 indicates Raising Awareness, a score of 3 indicates Skill-Building, and a score of 5 indicates Supporting Competence. Specific scoring anchors are provided for each of these levels, as well as for scores of 2 and 4. These anchors are designed to make the distinction between each level as concrete as possible.

The next section provides specific guidance for each item on the scored portion of the TIP Tool. For each item, a definition is provided, as well as descriptions of any terms used in the scoring instructions. Within the tool, key terms appear in bold at their first use, along with a definition. Specific guidance is then provided for coding each item, including a description of what constitutes a score at each level.

Training Information and Characteristics

Information to complete the section can be collected from the training director or manager, website, or other written training materials.

Training Program Identification

Definition: This section is intended to record basic information on the training and details on how to gain additional information. Raters should indicate the date the tool was completed and by whom.

Training Program Identification

Date __________ **Raters** ______________________________

Training Name ______________________________

Website ______________________________

Address ______________________________

Program Contact ______________________________

Telephone Number ______________________________

Email Address ______________________________

Training Characteristics

Definition: This section is intended to record the focus of the training, including the target psychotherapies and diagnoses, the size of the training, and whether there are any minimum qualifications required for clinicians (e.g., licensure in a mental health field, any prerequisite course completions). The section also gathers information about the format of the training.

- *Training format* refers to the way the training content is delivered. A rater should place a check mark next to "Available" after "In person" or "Web based" if any elements of the training are conducted in person or online, respectively. If the training features both optional and required components of a particular format (in person or web based), the rater should place a check mark in both boxes.
- *Typical length of didactic training* is the average number of hours required to complete the entire training. This number should include any required in-person and required web-based components, including training sessions, demonstrations, skill practice, discussion, and assessment. Optional components should **not** be included, such as reviewing supplemental materials, optional training components, time spent preparing for training sessions, or time spent on homework or outside skill practice. Supervision or consultation should also not be included.
- *Typical timing of didactic training* refers to the spacing of training sessions. If there is only one session, or if the training is conducted over several days without interruption, the rater should select "One time, consecutive days." If sessions take place over time, with breaks in between, the rater should select "Spaced out over time."

Training Characteristics

Target Psychotherapies Addressed by Training

____

____

____

____

____

Target Diagnoses Addressed by Training

____

____

____

____

____

Training Size

Number of trainings per year: ______

Average number of trainees per training: ______

Training Format

In person: ☐ Available ☐ Required

Web based: ☐ Available ☐ Required

Minimum Qualification of Trainees

____

____

____

____

____

____

Typical Length of Didactic Training

______ hours

Typical Timing of Didactic Training

☐ One time, consecutive days

☐ Spaced out over time

Scored Domains

The sections below and Tables 3.3–3.20 provide more detail on the definition and scoring for each of the scored domains. Although information to complete this section may be available in written materials, it may be necessary to gather the information directly from the training director, manager, or instructor.

Raters of each item must be familiar with the content of the training course and the way in which the training content is delivered. Raters should consider all recent (within six to 12 months) iterations of the training, including any variability caused by different training leaders or customizations made for trainees with different experience levels. Item scoring should account for this variability by endorsing the score that reflects how the training is typically delivered.

I. Didactic Training Format

IA. Length of Training

Definition: This is the total time required (in hours) to complete the entire training (not including breaks).

- This total *should* include the length of any required components of the training, including in-person or web-based training sessions and in-person or web-based demonstrations, skill practice, discussion, or assessment.
- This total should *not* include time spent on any of the following activities related to the training: supervision or consultation, reviewing supplemental materials, optional training components, time spent preparing for training sessions, or time spent on homework or outside skill practice.

Table 3.3
Item IA Response Options

	1 = Raising Awareness	2	3 = Skill-Building	4	5 = Supporting Competence
I. Didactic Training Format					
IA. Length of Training	2 hours or less	3 to 5 hours	6 to 8 hours	9 to 15 hours	16+ hours

Item Scoring:

- **Raising Awareness (1):** *2 hours or less.* The training is two hours or less in total length, such as a one-time two-hour workshop or a self-directed web-based course that requires an estimated two hours to complete.
- **(2):** *3 to 5 hours.* The training requires approximately three, four, or five hours to complete. Examples include a one-time five-hour workshop, a web-based facilitated training seminar completed in two sessions that are each two hours in length, or a self-directed web-based training that requires four to five hours to complete.
- **Skill-Building (3):** *6 to 8 hours.* The training requires approximately six, seven, or eight hours to complete. Examples include a daylong workshop, eight weekly hour-long training sessions, or a web-based seminar that takes an estimated eight hours to complete.
- **(4):** *9 to 15 hours.* The training is greater than or equal to nine hours and less than or equal to 15 hours in total length. Examples include two daylong workshops that are each seven hours in length, ten weekly hour-long training sessions, or a web-based training that takes approximately ten to 12 hours to complete.
- **Supporting Competence (5):** *16+ hours.* The training is 16 or more hours in total length. Examples include two daylong workshops that are each eight hours in length, ten weekly two-hour sessions, or a three-day workshop consisting of eight-hour training sessions.

IB. Level of Interactivity

Definition: This is the degree to which trainees interact with the training material through responding, reflecting, sharing, applying concepts, practicing skills, and otherwise engaging with the key concepts, theories, and skills featured in the training. Interactivity may take place in person or online.

- *Self-guided* trainings are facilitated by the trainee, and there is no training leader guiding either the in-person or web-based training session—nor are there any trainee peers with whom to interact (either online or in person). Self-guided formats include self-directed web-based programs, computer-based trainings, and self-guided training through the use of a training manual or guide.
- *Didactic* refers to the delivery of training content, such as theory or key concepts, through a lecture-style format in which the trainee is a listener and the training leader or web-based training program is the speaker or presenter of information.
- *Demonstrations* may be in person, online, or in a video. Demonstrations include any of the following activities: live demonstrations by the trainer, video demonstrations of relevant concepts or skills, web-based audiovisual demonstrations, and examples of concepts that are provided by trainees and confirmed by the training instructor for the benefit of the entire group of trainees.
- *Role play* is an exercise in which trainees practice using the skills and concepts featured in the training by interacting with a mock or simulated therapy client, either in person or online. The mock client might be a fellow trainee or group of trainees, the training leader, or a simulation. Role-play exercises might take place in pairs with no audience, or they may be conducted in "fishbowl" style in which the trainee(s) in the role play are observed by other trainees and/or the training leader.
- *Other interactive elements* (**not** demonstrations or role play) include
  - group discussion about interpretation, application, or understanding of training content, including discussion about a completed homework assignment
  - interactive quizzes or exercises (completed on paper, in person, or online) that require trainees to interact with the training content
  - games or activities (online or in person) in which trainees interact with one another to apply or learn the training material
  - contributions to peer discussion boards
  - case examples or vignettes presented by the training leader
  - skill practice during training (e.g., completing a thought record).

Table 3.4
Item IB Response Options

	1 = Raising Awareness	2	3 = Skill-Building	4	5 = Supporting Competence
I. Didactic Training Format					
IB. Level of Interactivity	Self-guided	**Didactic** only	Didactic, plus *either* **demonstrations** or **other interactive elements**	Didactic, plus *both* demonstrations and other interactive elements	Didactic, plus *all* of the following: demonstrations, other interactive elements, and **role plays**

Item Scoring:

- **Raising Awareness (1):** *Self-guided.* The trainee does not engage or interact directly with a training leader, nor does the trainee interact with trainee peers. Training content is delivered in a self-guided format, which may consist of a written or computer-based training manual, book, or online asynchronous web-based learning program that the trainee completes in his/her/their own time. An example of a training in this category is one that consists of a training manual plus quizzes on content.
- **(2):** *Didactic only.* There is little to no interaction between the trainee and the training leader, and there is little to no interaction with other trainees. Training content is delivered by a training leader either in person or online. The trainee listens but does not interact with the leader or content apart from asking clarifying questions.
- **Skill-Building (3):** *Didactic, plus* ***either*** *demonstrations or other interactive elements.* There is little to moderate interaction between the trainee and the training leader and/or trainee peers. Demonstrations (video or real-time) *or* other interactive elements are used to show a real-world application of the training content. The program uses a lecture format (in person or online) in which trainees listen at times without interacting, and it also features demonstrations or applications of relevant concepts or skills. The training does **not** include role play.
- **(4):** *Didactic, plus* ***both*** *demonstrations and other interactive elements.* There is moderate to significant interaction between the trainee and the training leader and/or trainee peers. The training uses a lecture format (in person or online) in which trainees listen at times without interacting, and it also features both demonstrations and applications of relevant concepts or skills. The training does **not** include role play.
- **Supporting Competence (5):** *Didactic, plus* ***all*** *of the following: demonstrations, other interactive elements, and role plays.* There is significant interaction between the trainee and the training leader and/or peers. The training uses a lecture format (in person or online) in which trainees listen at times without interacting, and it also features demonstrations, other applications of relevant concepts or skills, and role play.

IC. Individual Feedback During Training

Definition: This is information for the individual trainee conveyed during didactic training either aloud or in writing—and either in person or online—about individual learning, mastery, content knowledge, or skills pertaining to the training. Individual feedback is tailored in some way for the trainee; this item does not refer to feedback that might be given to the *entire group* of trainees.

- *Self-guided or self-generated feedback* is standardized, and it does not come from a person (e.g., trainer, peer). Examples include feedback generated from a self-assessment tool, tips identified through a training manual, and the results of a multiple-choice quiz.
- *Informal feedback* from the trainer or peer(s) refers to information that is shared (spoken or in writing) in an ad hoc fashion with the trainee. Examples include
  - observations or comments reflecting on trainee skill practice or role play
  - peer feedback during small-group discussion
  - reflections on a skill practice exercise conducted in pairs
  - leader comments on a homework assignment.
- *Structured feedback* uses a structured tool to provide feedback on strengths and opportunities for growth with regard to the course material. This feedback might pertain to performance (e.g., skill practice, role play) or to understanding of content. Examples include
  - graded or formal assessment on an assignment, exercise, or role play
  - use of a standard assessment to evaluate a role play or skill rehearsal.

Table 3.5
Item IC Response Options

	1 = Raising Awareness	2	3 = Skill-Building	4	5 = Supporting Competence
I. Didactic Training Format					
IC. Individual Feedback During Training	**Self-guided or self-generated** feedback only	Few trainees receive **informal** feedback from leader *or* peer(s)	Some but not all trainees receive informal feedback from leader *or* peer(s)	All trainees receive informal feedback from leader *or* peer(s)	**Structured,** individual feedback

Item Scoring:

- **Raising Awareness (1):** *Self-guided or self-generated only.* This type of feedback is standardized, and it does not come from a person.
- **(2):** *Few trainees receive informal feedback from leader* ***or*** *peer(s).* The feedback conveyed to trainee(s) is informal, meaning that it is delivered in an ad hoc manner in response to the trainee. One, two, or three trainees receive feedback.
- **Skill-Building (3):** *Some but not all trainees receive informal feedback from leader* ***or*** *peer(s).* More than three but fewer than all trainees receive feedback. The feedback (spoken or written) conveyed to trainees is informal, meaning that it is delivered in an ad hoc manner in response to the trainee.
- **(4):** *All trainees receive informal feedback from leader* ***or*** *peer(s).* The feedback (spoken or written) conveyed to trainee(s) is informal, meaning that it is delivered in an ad hoc manner in response to the trainee. A training that scores a 4 on this item likely cre-

ates multiple opportunities to deliver feedback so that, over time, every trainee has the opportunity to receive comments from the leader or peer(s). For example, role plays could include another trainee who serves as an observer and provides feedback following the role-play exercise.

- **Supporting Competence (5):** *Structured, individual feedback.* All trainees in the training receive individual feedback from the training leader(s), either spoken or written. The purpose of the feedback is to evaluate the trainee's understanding or apparent mastery of training content by providing information about particular strengths or opportunities for improvement.

ID. Integration of Written Materials

Definition: This is the extent to which print resources are used and integrated in the training.

- *Written materials* include training manuals or guides, books, handouts generated from a book or manual, and handouts developed specifically for the training, as well as the availability of these materials online or through a computer program. This does not refer to printouts of briefing slides used in the training but instead refers to supplemental resources.

Table 3.6
Item ID Response Options

	1 = Raising Awareness	2	3 = Skill-Building	4	5 = Supporting Competence
I. Didactic Training Format					
ID. Integration of Written Materials	**No use of written materials**	Written materials provided but not integrated into didactic training	Review of written materials suggested before or after didactic training	Review of written materials strongly encouraged but not required	Review of written materials required before or after didactic training

Item Scoring:

- **Raising Awareness (1):** *No use of written materials.* The training does not use or suggest that trainees use any materials, such as manuals, guides, books, or handouts. A training with this score does not offer any optional materials through an online platform or computer program.
- **(2):** *Written materials provided but not integrated into didactic training.* The training may provide access to written materials, but this resource is not mentioned during training, nor is it suggested as a helpful prerequisite. A training with this score might list an optional text in a syllabus without mentioning it during the course, or it might post supplemental materials online for trainees to access based on interest.
- **Skill-Building (3):** *Review of written materials suggested before or after didactic training.* The training suggests that trainees access written materials before or after the didactic training, but it does not require it. The trainer might reference the availability or possible use of materials during the training, but the materials are not discussed at length or in great detail.
- **(4):** *Review of written materials strongly encouraged but not required.* The training encourages trainees to access written materials before or after the training. Although use or review of the materials is not a requirement, there is a sincere attempt on the part of the training leader to encourage trainees to do so. The leader might mention the availability of such resources more than once during the training, and there is likely an opportunity to discuss or review material related to these resources during the didactic training.
- **Supporting Competence (5):** *Review of written materials required before or after didactic training.* A training meeting this score has a stated requirement involving a training manual, book, or other written resource that trainees are required to review or use as a part of the training. The requirement need not be enforced through an exam or other measure, but it must be a stated requirement of the training such that the majority of trainees do make use of these resources.

II. Didactic Training Content

IIA. Core Techniques and Theory

Definition: This is the extent to which the didactic training content includes and covers the theoretical underpinnings and central therapeutic techniques of the psychotherapy on which the training is focused. This item pertains to didactic training content only, **not** consultation/supervision.

- *Concepts* refers to core techniques and/or theory:
  - *Core techniques* are the actual methods or processes by which a clinician delivers a psychotherapy. Examples of techniques include in vivo exposure, relaxation training, cognitive restructuring, behavioral experiments, activity monitoring/scheduling, and using a Subjective Units of Distress Scale.
  - *Theory* is an explanation of how the psychotherapy helps patients change. For example, a training that covers the theory of CBT would explain how thoughts and behaviors relate to mood.
- *Supplemental materials* include training manuals or guides; books; course handouts; such resources as videos, graphics, websites, or reports that are posted to a website or available through a computer program; and anything else that is provided to trainees for review outside of the didactic training.

Table 3.7
Item IIA Response Options

	1 = Raising Awareness	2	3 = Skill-Building	4	5 = Supporting Competence
II. Didactic Training Content					
IIA. Core Techniques and Theory	Not included	Concepts addressed in **supplemental materials** or resources but not discussed in didactic training	Concepts introduced in didactic training	Concepts discussed with examples in didactic training	Trainees given opportunity to practice or apply concepts in didactic training

Item Scoring:

- **Raising Awareness (1):** *Not included.* The training does not include any of the core techniques or theory during didactic training, nor does it provide any resources on these topics.
- **(2):** *Concepts addressed in supplemental materials or resources but not discussed in didactic training.* The training provides materials or resources that mention core techniques and theory, but they are not discussed during didactic training.
- **Skill-Building (3):** *Concepts introduced in didactic training.* At least one core technique and at least one aspect of theory is explicitly mentioned during didactic training without going into depth with examples. These components might be mentioned only once, or they might be mentioned more than once without any applied examples. Trainees do not have the opportunity to practice or apply information on this topic.
- **(4):** *Concepts discussed with examples in didactic training.* Technique and theory are introduced and explicitly discussed with applied examples for either or both components

during didactic training. There are no opportunities to practice the techniques or apply concepts of theory through role play or any other applied method.

- **Supporting Competence (5):** *Trainees given opportunity to practice or apply concepts in didactic training.* The training provides explicit instruction on both core techniques and theory during didactic training, including applied examples. Trainees are given the opportunity to practice or apply the concepts that are discussed. Practice might take the form of a role-play or skill exercise, or trainees in small groups might discuss hypothetical scenarios and the way they would respond. In general, the examples and the exploration of the material that are provided during training are relatively in depth and detailed. The training does not necessarily cover all aspects of theory and techniques for the psychotherapy of focus, but it likely touches on more than one aspect of each.

IIB. Clinical Judgment and Decisionmaking

Definition: This is the extent to which the didactic training content includes instruction about clinical decisionmaking with the psychotherapy of focus or how to decide what to do during a psychotherapy session. This item pertains to didactic training content only, **not** consultation/supervision.

- *Supplemental materials* include training manuals or guides; books; course handouts; such resources as videos, graphics, websites, or reports that are posted to a website or available through a computer program; and anything else that is provided to trainees for review outside of the didactic training period.

Table 3.8
Item IIB Response Options

	1 = Raising Awareness	2	3 = Skill-Building	4	5 = Supporting Competence
II. Didactic Training Content					
IIB. Clinical Judgment and Decisionmaking	Not included	Concepts addressed in supplemental materials or resources but not discussed in didactic training	Concepts introduced in didactic training	Concepts discussed with examples in didactic training	Trainees given opportunity to practice or apply concepts in didactic training

Item Scoring:

- **Raising Awareness (1):** *Not included.* The training does not cover the topic of clinical judgment and decisionmaking during didactic training, nor does it provide any resources on this topic.
- **(2):** *Concepts addressed in supplemental materials or resources but not discussed in didactic training.* The training provides materials or resources that mention the concept of clinical judgment and decisionmaking using the EBP of focus, but this topic is neither discussed nor practiced during didactic training.
- **Skill-Building (3):** *Concepts introduced in didactic training.* The training explicitly mentions the concept of clinical judgment and decisionmaking during didactic training without going into depth with examples. Trainees do not have the opportunity to practice or apply information on this topic.
- **(4):** *Concepts discussed with examples in didactic training.* Clinical decisionmaking is introduced and explicitly discussed with applied examples during the didactic training. There are no opportunities for trainees to practice or apply information on this topic.
- **Supporting Competence (5):** *Trainees given opportunity to practice or apply concepts in didactic training.* The training provides explicit instruction on clinical decisionmaking during didactic training, including applied examples. Trainees are given the opportunity to practice or apply the concepts that are discussed. Practice might take the form of a role play or skill exercise, or trainees might discuss in small groups a series of hypothetical scenarios and the way they might respond based on the information provided during the training.

IIC. Addressing Co-Occurring Disorders

Definition: This is the extent to which the didactic training content includes instruction about addressing co-occurring disorders with the psychotherapy of focus. This item pertains to didactic training content only, **not** consultation/supervision.

- *Supplemental materials* include training manuals or guides; books; course handouts; such resources as videos, graphics, websites, or reports that are posted to a website or available through a computer program; and anything else that is provided to trainees for review outside of the didactic training period.

Table 3.9
Item IIC Response Options

	1 = Raising Awareness	2	3 = Skill-Building	4	5 = Supporting Competence
II. Didactic Training Content					
IIC. Addressing Co-Occurring Disorders	Not included	Concept addressed in supplemental materials or resources but not discussed in didactic training	Concept introduced in didactic training	Concept discussed with examples in didactic training	Trainees given opportunity to practice or apply concept in didactic training

Item Scoring:

- **Raising Awareness (1):** *Not included.* The training does not include the topic of co-occurring disorders during didactic training, nor does it provide any resources on this topic.
- **(2):** *Concept addressed in supplemental materials or resources but not discussed in didactic training.* The training provides materials or resources that mention the concept of treating co-occurring disorders with the psychotherapy of focus, but this topic is neither discussed nor practiced during didactic training.
- **Skill-Building (3):** *Concept introduced in didactic training.* The training explicitly mentions the concept of treating co-occurring disorders with the psychotherapy of focus during didactic training without going into depth with examples. Trainees do not have the opportunity to practice or apply information on this topic.
- **(4):** *Concept discussed with examples in didactic training.* Addressing co-occurring disorders with the psychotherapy of focus is explicitly discussed with applied examples during didactic training. There are no opportunities for trainees to practice or apply information on this topic.
- **Supporting Competence (5):** *Trainees given opportunity to practice or apply concept in didactic training.* The training provides explicit instruction on addressing co-occurring disorders with the psychotherapy of focus during didactic training, including applied examples. Trainees are given the opportunity to practice or apply the concepts that are discussed. Practice might take the form of a role-play or skill exercise, or trainees might discuss in small groups a hypothetical case formulation and the way they might treat that client differently from how they might treat someone without co-occurring conditions, based on the information provided during the training.

IID. Measurement-Based Care

Definition: This is the extent to which the didactic training content includes the topic of measurement-based care. Measurement-based care is the systematic administration of symptom measures and use of the information from these measures to inform clinical decisionmaking at the individual patient level (Fortney et al., 2016). This item pertains to didactic training content only, **not** consultation/supervision.

- *Supplemental materials* include training manuals or guides; books; course handouts; such resources as videos, graphics, websites, or reports that are posted to a website or available through a computer program; and anything else that is provided to trainees for review outside of the didactic training period.

Table 3.10
Item IID Response Options

	1 = Raising Awareness	2	3 = Skill-Building	4	5 = Supporting Competence
II. Didactic Training Content					
IID. Measurement-Based Care	Not included	Concept addressed in supplemental materials or resources but not discussed in didactic training	Concept introduced in didactic training	Concept discussed with examples in didactic training	Trainees given opportunity to practice or apply concept in didactic training

Item Scoring:

- **Raising Awareness (1):** *Not included.* The training does not include the topic of measurement-based care during didactic training, nor does it provide any resources on this topic.
- **(2):** *Concept addressed in supplemental materials or resources but not discussed in didactic training.* The training provides materials or resources that mention the concept of measurement-based care, but this topic is neither discussed nor practiced during didactic training.
- **Skill-Building (3):** *Concept introduced in didactic training.* The training explicitly mentions the concept of measurement-based care during didactic training without going into depth with examples. Trainees do not have the opportunity to practice or apply information on this topic.
- **(4):** *Concept discussed with examples in didactic training.* Measurement-based care is explicitly discussed with applied examples during didactic training. There are no opportunities for trainees to practice or apply information on this topic.
- **Supporting Competence (5):** *Trainees given opportunity to practice or apply concept in didactic training.* The training provides explicit instruction on measurement-based care during didactic training (e.g., selecting appropriate measures, frequency of administering measures, how to use the data to adjust treatment), including applied examples. Trainees are given the opportunity to practice or apply the concepts that are discussed. Practice might take the form of a role-play or skill exercise, or trainees might discuss in small groups a hypothetical case and strategies to integrate measurement-based care based on

the information provided during the training (e.g., ways to discuss treatment progress with patients using measurement-based care data).

III. Consultation/Supervision

IIIA. Availability of Consultation/Supervision

Definition: This is the extent to which the training offers consultation or supervision. Supervision or consultation typically involves an expert in the modality providing support, guidance, and critical feedback to the trainee. Consultation/supervision may be conducted in person or via telephone, videoconference, or webinar or as group or individual supervision.

Table 3.11
Item IIIA Response Options

	1 = Raising Awareness	2	3 = Skill-Building	4	5 = Supporting Competence
III. Consultation/Supervision					
IIIA. Availability of Consultation/Supervision	Not referenced	Consultation/supervision (from training or training partner) is referenced during didactic training	Consultation/supervision (from training or training partner) is available and is suggested	Consultation/supervision (from training or training partner) is available and is encouraged	Consultation/supervision (from training or training partner) is available and is required

Item Scoring:

- **Raising Awareness (1):** *Not referenced.* The training does not mention supervision during didactic training.
- **(2):** *Consultation/supervision (from training or training partner) is referenced during didactic training.* The training leader might mention consultation/supervision aloud, or an online training might contain a written reference to consultation/supervision, but trainees are **not** prompted to consider whether they might want to seek consultation/supervision.
- **Skill-Building (3):** *Consultation/supervision (from training or training partner) is available and is suggested.* The training suggests that trainees might seek consultation/supervision, either provided by the training or through a training partner. The training does **not** try to persuade trainees to seek consultation/supervision, but it is referenced as an option.
- **(4):** *Consultation/supervision (from training or training partner) is available and is encouraged.* The training attempts to persuade trainees to seek consultation/supervision, but it is not a requirement.
- **Supporting Competence (5):** *Consultation/supervision (from training or training partner) is available and is required.* Every trainee in the program is required to complete consultation/supervision.

IIIB. Review of Sessions

Definition: This is encouragement or requirement for the review of therapy sessions as part of the consultation or supervision component of the training.

- *Trainee therapy sessions* are those sessions conducted by the trainee with an actual client. Recordings or reports of practice sessions with mock or simulated patients are not to be included in rater assessment and scoring of this item.

Table 3.12
Item IIIB Response Options

	1 = Raising Awareness	2	3 = Skill-Building	4	5 = Supporting Competence
III. Consultation/Supervision					
IIIB. Review of Sessions	Not available	Formal review of **trainee therapy sessions** is not provided but is suggested	Written or spoken self-report of trainee therapy session(s) reviewed	Live or recorded trainee therapy session(s) reviewed and evaluated without a structured coding tool	Live or recorded therapy session(s) reviewed and evaluated using a structured coding tool

Item Scoring:

- **Raising Awareness (1):** *Not available.* The training does not offer review of recorded therapy sessions by a clinical supervisor, nor does it suggest or encourage trainees to seek outside supervision for review of recorded therapy sessions.
- **(2):** *Formal review of trainee therapy sessions is not provided but is suggested.* The training encourages trainees to seek outside supervision for review of recorded or therapy sessions.
- **Skill-Building (3):** *Written or spoken self-report of trainee therapy session(s) reviewed.* The training provides review of written or spoken self-report of trainee therapy session(s) as a part of the training. This review process can take place in person, over the phone, or by videoconference. The supervisor might provide a written or spoken evaluation of the trainee or may use a standardized tool to provide feedback to the trainee, but an evaluative component is not required to receive a score of 3.
- **(4):** *Live or recorded trainee therapy session(s) reviewed and evaluated without a structured coding tool.* The training provides review of live or recorded trainee therapy session(s), and this review is accompanied by an unstructured evaluative component.
- **Supporting Competence (5):** *Live or recorded therapy session(s) reviewed and evaluated using a structured coding tool.* The training provides an evaluation of live or recorded trainee therapy session(s), giving feedback to trainees using a structured coding tool.

IIIC. Supervision Length

Definition: This is the provision of trainee supervision or consultation as a component of training.

Table 3.13
Item IIIC Response Options

	1 = Raising Awareness	2	3 = Skill-Building	4	5 = Supporting Competence
III. Consultation/Supervision					
IIIC. Supervision Length	No consultation/ supervision provided	Consultation/ supervision provided, but no specified length or case target	Consultation/ supervision provided for at least two months	Consultation/ supervision provided for at least six months or until trainee demonstrates adherence and competence with one patient	Consultation/ supervision provided and continues until trainee demonstrates adherence and competence in session with at least two patients

Item Scoring:

- **Raising Awareness (1):** *No consultation/supervision provided.* Consultation/supervision might be mentioned, suggested, or even encouraged by the training, but it is not a requirement.
- **(2):** *Consultation/supervision provided, but no specified length or case target.* There is no minimum length of time or number of client cases required for consultation/supervision.
- **Skill-Building (3):** *Consultation/supervision provided for at least two months.* The training requires a minimum of two months of consultation/supervision, either provided by a partner training or facilitated by the training itself.
- **(4):** *Consultation/supervision provided for at least six months or until trainee demonstrates adherence and competence with one patient.* The training requires a minimum of six months of consultation/supervision, either provided by the training organization or facilitated by the training itself, unless the trainee demonstrates adherence and competence before six months. Trainees must achieve adherence and competence with one patient, based on an assessment of trainee live or recorded therapy sessions using a structured coding tool. Though some trainings may require completion of a certain number of training cases, for trainings offering less than six months of supervision to obtain this score, there must be assessment of adherence and competence with those training cases.
- **Supporting Competence (5):** *Consultation/supervision provided and continues until trainee demonstrates adherence and competence in session with at least two patients.* The training requires that a trainee continues in consultation/supervision until achieving adherence and competence with two patients, based on an assessment of trainee live or recorded therapy sessions using a structured coding tool.

IIID. Certification

Definition: This is encouragement or requirement of trainee certification as a part of the training.

- *Certification* in a psychotherapy typically indicates that the clinician has demonstrated an ability to deliver the psychotherapy with fidelity. An example of a certification program is the Academy of Cognitive Therapy, which certifies clinicians in CBT. These are distinct from licensure and other certification or credentialing programs that do not include an assessment of fidelity to the psychotherapy.

Table 3.14
Item IIID Response Options

	1 = Raising Awareness	2	3 = Skill-Building	4	5 = Supporting Competence
III. Consultation/Supervision					
IIID. Certification	Training does not mention certification to trainees	Supplemental materials or resources mention certification but not discussed in didactic training	Certification is mentioned during training or supervision as an option	Certification is encouraged	Certification is strongly encouraged, and training tracks the number of trainees who receive certification

Item Scoring:

- **Raising Awareness (1):** *Training does not mention certification to trainees.*
- **(2):** *Supplemental materials or resources mention certification but not discussed in didactic training.* Supplemental materials might include handouts or online resources.
- **Skill-Building (3):** *Certification is mentioned during training or supervision as an option.* Trainees are neither required nor encouraged by the training to pursue certification.
- **(4):** *Certification is encouraged.* Certification is mentioned during didactic training or supervision as an option, and trainees are encouraged to think about obtaining certification upon completion of the training.
- **Supporting Competence (5):** *Certification is strongly encouraged, and training tracks the number of trainees who receive certification.* Certification is the ultimate goal of the training. Although not all trainees may be certified, it is strongly encouraged, and the training tracks the number of trainees who receive certification.

IV. Program Evaluation

IVA. Course Evaluation

Definition: This is an assessment of the trainee experience and satisfaction with the training and the extent to which any information collected is used to improve the training.

Table 3.15
Item IVA Response Options

	1 = Raising Awareness	2	3 = Skill-Building	4	5 = Supporting Competence
IV. Program Evaluation					
IVA. Course Evaluation	No course evaluation of the training	Optional course evaluation or other opportunity to share trainee feedback with the training	Required assessment of trainee experience with the training	Information from the required assessment of trainee experience with the training is routinely shared with trainers	Information from the required assessment of trainee experience with training is used to improve training content, format, and facilitation

Item Scoring:

- **Raising Awareness (1):** *No course evaluation of the training.* The training does not provide opportunity for trainees to give any formal feedback or course evaluation.
- **(2):** *Optional course evaluation or other opportunity to share trainee feedback with the training.* The training leader or training staff express a willingness to receive feedback.
- **Skill-Building (3):** *Required assessment of trainee experience with the training.* The training collects trainee feedback, but the information is not routinely shared with trainers, nor is it used to improve the training.
- **(4):** *Information from the required assessment of trainee experience with the training is routinely shared with trainers.* Although the training leaders are informed of trainee feedback, this information is not otherwise used to improve the training.
- **Supporting Competence (5):** *Information from the required assessment of trainee experience with training is used to improve training content, format, and facilitation.* Not only is the information about trainee feedback routinely shared with training leaders, but the training also responds by making significant and regular (e.g., annual) improvements in response to trainee feedback.

IVB. Knowledge

Definition: This is an assessment of trainee knowledge related to the psychotherapy of focus.

- An assessment of *perceived knowledge* asks the trainee to estimate how much they have learned about the psychotherapy (e.g., participant ratings of the extent to which participation in the training led to an increase in knowledge). Perceived knowledge tests are coded by the training to determine the trainee's self-reported perceived level of knowledge about the psychotherapy.
- A knowledge *test* assesses understanding of key concepts and techniques. Unlike tests of perceived knowledge, tests of knowledge are graded by the training to determine the trainee's actual, objective level of knowledge about the psychotherapy.

Table 3.16
Item IVB Response Options

	1 = Raising Awareness	2	3 = Skill-Building	4	5 = Supporting Competence
IV. Program Evaluation					
IVB. Knowledge	No assessment of trainee knowledge	Brief post-training assessment (5 items or fewer) of **trainee-perceived knowledge** change	Post-training assessment of trainee-perceived knowledge change	Post-training test of trainee knowledge	Pre- and post-training test of trainee knowledge

Item Scoring:

- **Raising Awareness (1):** *No assessment of trainee knowledge.*
- **(2):** *Brief post-training assessment (five items or fewer) of trainee-perceived knowledge change.* There may or may not be a pre-course assessment of perceived trainee knowledge.
- **Skill-Building (3):** *Post-training assessment of trainee-perceived knowledge change.* The training asks trainees to reflect on whether their knowledge about the psychotherapy has changed. There may or may not be a pre-course assessment of perceived trainee knowledge (e.g., "How knowledgeable are you about creating thought records?"). The training does **not** administer a knowledge test (e.g., "Which of the following is a definition of an automatic thought?").
- **(4):** *Post-training test of trainee knowledge.* There is no pre-test or baseline assessment. The training may or may not ask trainees about perceived knowledge, but it must assess knowledge using a test that is scored by the training leader.
- **Supporting Competence (5):** *Pre- and post-training test of trainee knowledge.* Trainees complete a test related to the training content both before and after the training so that pre/post scores can be compared to determine change over time. The training may or may not ask trainees about perceived knowledge, but it must assess knowledge using a test that is scored by the training leader.

IVC. Skills

Definition: This is an assessment of trainee skills related to the psychotherapy of focus.

Table 3.17
Item IVC Response Options

	1 = Raising Awareness	2	3 = Skill-Building	4	5 = Supporting Competence
IV. Program Evaluation					
IVC. Skills	No assessment of trainee skills	Post-training assessment of trainee-perceived skills	Post-training assessment of trainee-perceived ability to use specific skills	Post-training assessment of trainee self-reported confidence in applying specific skills	Post-training assessment of trainee ability to use specific skills (e.g., role play)

Item Scoring:

- **Raising Awareness (1):** *No assessment of trainee skills.* The training does not provide any assessment of trainee skills related to the psychotherapy of focus.
- **(2):** *Post-training assessment of trainee-perceived therapeutic skills included in training.* The training asks the trainee to indicate which therapeutic skills were included in the training content. These questions might be incorporated in a questionnaire about satisfaction with the training or asked independently as a measure of what skills trainees recall learning during the training. The training does **not** ask the trainees about their perceived ability to use the therapeutic skill(s).
- **Skill-Building (3):** *Post-training assessment of trainee-perceived ability to use specific therapeutic skills.* The training asks the trainee to report their perceived ability to use therapeutic skills associated with the psychotherapy of focus. For example, a post-training assessment for a cognitive processing therapy training might ask trainees whether they know how to work with a client to identify stuck points. The training does not ask the trainees about how confident they are in their ability to use the therapeutic skill(s).
- **(4):** *Post-training assessment of trainee self-reported confidence in applying specific therapeutic skills.* The training asks trainees to estimate how well they think they might do with applying therapeutic skill(s) during psychotherapy with a client.
- **Supporting Competence (5):** *Post-training assessment of trainee ability to use the specific therapeutic skills (e.g., role play).* Rather than asking the trainee to report on their perceived learning, ability, or confidence, the training uses an objective test to evaluate trainee therapeutic skill that is facilitated through a role play or similar exercise.

V. Implementation Facilitation

VA. Development of an Implementation Plan

Definition: These are activities to assist clinicians in planning for the incorporation of new knowledge and skills into their clinical practice.

Table 3.18
Item VA Response Options

	1 = Raising Awareness	2	3 = Skill-Building	4	5 = Supporting Competence
V. Implementation Facilitation					
VA. Development of a Plan for Implementation	Not present	Course materials or didactic training references indicate that trainees should consider developing a plan for implementation	Course materials or didactic training describes how to develop a plan for implementation	Training provides time for clinicians to develop a basic plan for implementation	Training includes the development of a comprehensive plan for implementation

Item Scoring:

- **Raising Awareness (1):** *Not present.* There is no mention of developing a plan for implementing the psychotherapy into the trainee's clinical practice.
- **(2):** *Course materials or didactic training indicates that trainees should consider developing a plan for implementation.* This indication could be made through written materials or written communication or could be spoken aloud during the didactic training.
- **Skill-Building (3):** *Course materials or didactic training indicates how to develop a plan for implementation.* The training uses course materials that describe the development of an implementation plan, or it describes this concept during didactic training without providing specific suggestions about strategies for developing this type of plan. Trainees might have access to a template that could be used to develop an implementation that they could complete on their own, but there is no facilitated completion of such a plan during didactic training.
- **(4):** *Training provides time for the clinician to develop a basic plan for implementation.* The training provides time for trainees to begin developing a basic plan for implementation. For example, trainees may be asked to consider one or two practice changes they could commit to making in the immediate future. The nature of these practice changes and level of detail are left to the trainee.
- **Supporting Competence (5):** *Training includes the development of a comprehensive plan for implementation.* The training provides time for trainees to develop a comprehensive plan for implementation. Trainees are guided to consider not only practice changes they will make in the near term but also any challenges they may encounter and ways to address those issues. Trainees may be provided with a structured way to develop this plan, such as a worksheet or implementation plan template.

VB. Assessment of Organizational Context

Definition: This is the amount of instruction and guidance on the assessment of organizational context that is provided by the training.

Table 3.19
Item VB Response Options

	1 = Raising Awareness	2	3 = Skill-Building	4	5 = Supporting Competence
V. Implementation Facilitation					
VB. Assessment of Organizational Context	Not present	Course materials or didactic training references indicate that organizational context should be considered	Course materials or didactic training describes how to assess organizational context, including potential barriers to implementation	Course materials or didactic training provides specific suggestions for overcoming implementation barriers	Training includes a structured assessment plan to identify potential barriers and solutions at trainee's site

Item Scoring:

- **Raising Awareness (1):** *Not present.* There is no mention of the role of organizational context or setting in supporting or hindering implementation of a new psychotherapy approach.
- **(2):** *Course materials or didactic training indicates that organizational context should be considered.* This indication could be made through written materials or during the didactic training.
- **Skill-Building (3):** *Course materials or didactic training indicates how to assess organizational context, including potential barriers to implementation.* The training uses course materials that describe assessment for organizational context, or it describes this concept during didactic training without providing specific suggestions about strategies for overcoming particular barriers. Trainees might have access to an assessment for organizational context that they could complete on their own, but there is no facilitated completion or review of such an assessment during didactic training.
- **(4):** *Course materials or didactic training provides specific suggestions for overcoming implementation barriers.* The training might facilitate an agency assessment before the training, or it might instruct trainees on how to complete such assessments in their respective agencies during didactic training. The training does **not** provide concrete suggestions for overcoming barriers at trainees' respective implementation sites.
- **Supporting Competence (5):** *Training includes a structured assessment plan to identify potential barriers and solutions at trainee's site.* The training provides specific guidance on barriers to implementation during at least two of the following phases: before, during, and after the didactic training. The solutions provided to the trainee are specific to their individual implementation sites.

VC. Implementation Support

Definition: This is the amount of support for implementation of the psychotherapy that is available through the training.

- *Outside resources* include any of the following:
  - websites or links to information online
  - recommended training manuals, guides, books, or other written materials
  - a list of recommended agencies or institutions that support implementation.

Table 3.20
Item VC Response Options

	1 = Raising Awareness	2	3 = Skill-Building	4	5 = Supporting Competence
V. Implementation Facilitation					
VC. Implementation Support	Not available	Implementation support is not available, but self-guided use of **outside resources** is suggested	Brief implementation consultation is available from the training	Implementation support is available from the training	Full implementation support is available from the training before and after didactic training

Item Scoring:

- **Raising Awareness (1):** *Not available.* There is no support available for implementation.
- **(2):** *Implementation support is not available, but self-guided use of outside resources is suggested.* The training identifies specific resources that trainees might use to support implementation.
- **Skill-Building (3):** *Brief implementation consultation is available from the training.* The training provides limited support for implementation, possibly through both the provision of outside resources and direct guidance to trainees or to their respective organizations.
- **(4):** *Implementation support is available from the training.* The training provides support for implementation at one time point only: before, during, or after didactic training.
- **Supporting Competence (5):** *Full implementation support is available from the training before and after didactic training.* The training provides support for implementation during at least two of the following phases: before, during, and after the didactic training.

Scoring Guidance

Scores on individual items should be selected based on the best available information about the training. The total sum is calculated by summing the raw item scores for the 18 items in each of the five domain sections I through V: Didactic Training Format (items A–D), Didactic Training Content (items A–D), Consultation/Supervision (items A–D), Program Evaluation (items A–C), and Implementation Facilitation (items A–C). The total sum will range between 18 and 90 (see Table 3.21). The TIP score is calculated by dividing the total sum by 18. TIP scores will range between 1 and 5, or between Raising Awareness (1) and Supporting Compe-

Table 3.21
TIP Tool Scoring Summary

Domain	Number of Items	Domain Sum Range	Domain Score Range
I. Didactic Training Format	4	4–20	1–5
II. Didactic Training Content	4	4–20	1–5
III. Consultation/Supervision	4	4–20	1–5
IV. Program Evaluation	3	3–15	1–5
V. Implementation Facilitation	3	3–15	1–5
		Total Sum Range	**TIP Score Range**
Overall score	18	18–90	1–5

NOTE: As described above, each domain score is calculated by dividing the domain sum by the number of items for that domain; the overall TIP score is calculated by dividing the total sum by the total number of items.

tence (5). The overall TIP total score should be used to determine the corresponding TIP score category (Raising Awareness, Skill-Building, or Supporting Competence). A TIP total score of 1.00 to 2.33 corresponds to Raising Awareness, a total score of 2.34 to 3.66 corresponds to Skill-Building, and a total score of 3.67 to 5.00 corresponds to Supporting Competence. The domain sums and scores in each section may provide more-specific feedback about the strengths and opportunities for program changes. Each domain sum is calculated by summing the raw item scores for the items within that domain. Domain sums will range between 4 and 20 for Didactic Training Format, Didactic Training Content, and Consultation/Supervision. The domain sum for Program Evaluation will range between 3 and 15, and the section sum for Implementation Facilitation will range between 3 and 15. The more informative TIP domain score is calculated by dividing the domain sum by the total number of items in that section, as specified on the scoring sheet. TIP domain scores will range between 1 and 5, or between Raising Awareness (1) and Supporting Competence (5). Each domain score should be used to determine the corresponding domain score category (Raising Awareness, Skill-Building, or Supporting Competence). A domain score of 1.00 to 2.33 corresponds to Raising Awareness, a domain score of 2.34 to 3.66 corresponds to Skill-Building, and a domain score of 3.67 to 5.00 corresponds to Supporting Competence.

After calculating the domain and overall scores, the results can be plotted on the TIP Tool scoring template. An example template that has been completed appears in Figure 3.1, and a blank template is included in Appendix C. Plotting the results can assist in the interpretation of TIP Tool scores. For example, the training characterized in Figure 3.1 scores a 4.5 for Didactic Training Format, which falls into the Supporting Competence range, whereas the scores for Didactic Training Content and Program Evaluation fall into the Skill-Building range. The score for Consultation/Supervision is at the top end of the Raising Awareness range; this information may be of use to the organizers of the training because making even small changes to the supervision component of the training may help the program move up into the Skill-Building range. Because this training does not address implementation, its score in the Implementation Facilitation falls into the bottom of the Raising Awareness range. This may be appropriate, given the focus or resources of the training; alternatively, the organizers could use the scoring anchors for the items in this category to gain ideas on how they might achieve

Figure 3.1
TIP Tool Scores

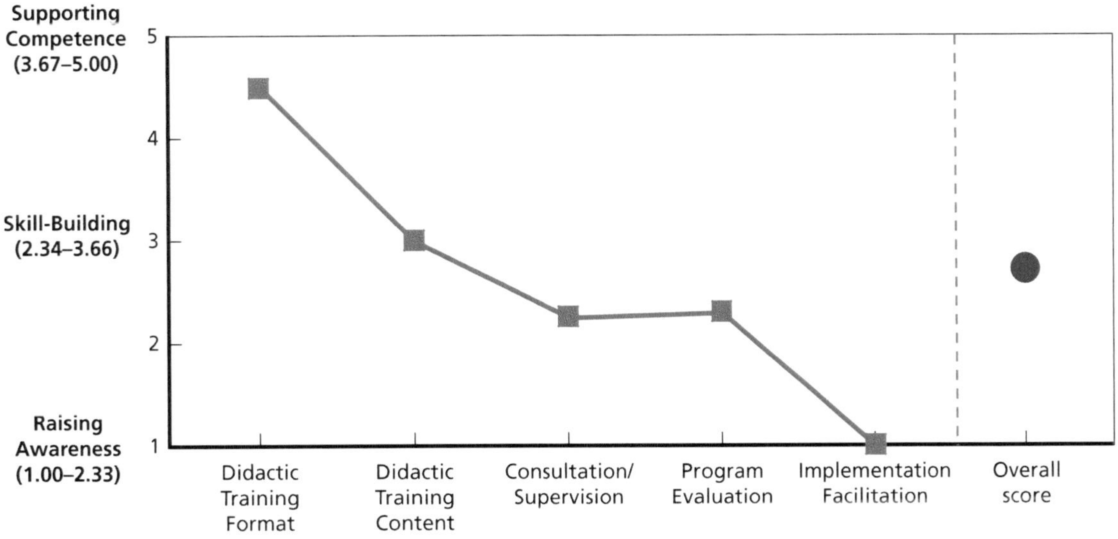

RAND *TL306-3.1*

a higher score in this domain. Finally, the overall score for the program is in the Skill-Building range. Depending on the way the organization plans to use the scores from this tool, this may be helpful information. For example, the organization leadership can determine whether this score is consistent with their goal for the program. If not, an examination of the domain scores will provide more concrete guidance as to changes that could be made to the training.

Summary

This chapter provided an overview of the TIP Tool, including potential users and uses of the TIP Tool, as well as ways that the tool could be used to assess a training (i.e., based on a representative training, capabilities than an organization can offer, or applied to specific trainings). It also provided detailed instructions for scoring each item on the tool and deriving domain and total scores.

It is important to note that the interpretation of the domain and total scores will vary based on the goal of the training. As described previously, some trainings may have the goal of raising awareness. These trainings provide an overview of a given psychotherapy, such as the underlying theory and key clinical techniques, but might not intend to help therapists achieve competence or adherence. For these trainings, domain and total scores toward the lower end of the 1–5 range are consistent with the goals of the training. Similarly, although some training leaders/organizations may be interested in their scores on all domains of the tool, as well as the total score, others may be interested in interpreting specific domain scores. For example, leaders/organizers of a training that is not designed to provide supervision or facilitate implementation of a given psychotherapy may be less interested in their scores on Domains IV and V and may opt not to interpret the total score, instead focusing on scores for Domains I, II, and III. In this way, the TIP Tool is designed to be applicable to a broad range of trainings and users.

In the final chapter, we provide a summary of the TIP Tool development process and highlight next steps for the evaluation of this tool, as well as ways a tool of this nature could be used to promote the dissemination and implementation of evidence-based psychotherapies.

CHAPTER FOUR

Summary and Next Steps

This report has described the initial development of the TIP Tool. The tool was developed following a literature review and consultation with selected experts to identify core elements of effective psychotherapy training. A draft of the TIP Tool was reviewed by additional experts, and the tool was revised in response to these reviews.

Given the early stage of development of the TIP Tool, some limitations should be noted. Although domain selection, item development, and scoring guidance were informed by available literature and expert input, the literature did not fully address the utility of each element included in the tool. In addition, the literature was not sufficiently detailed to fully inform our detailed scoring criteria. When there was a gap in the literature, our team used judgment and expert consultation to inform tool development. For example, it is possible that some elements assessed by the tool are more important than others in terms of their relationship with clinician fidelity to an EBP. In the absence of clear guidance from the literature on the relative importance of various elements, we used a scoring approach that equally weighted all elements. Although we considered differential weighting, the literature did not provide clear guidance to support differential weighting at this time. In addition, tools and measures do not use differential item weighting due to increased scoring complexity for the end user and the risk of conveying increased precision that is not well supported by the empirical literature (Wang and Stanley, 1970). Further, although we considered how various trainings might score on individual items, we did not conduct formal pilot testing of the TIP Tool on specific trainings. Therefore, the usability and utility of the tool to characterize trainings still needs to be demonstrated.

Next Steps in Evaluation and Validation of the TIP Tool

The TIP Tool will require additional development and testing to inform future revisions and evaluate its utility.

Further development of the TIP Tool will involve applying the tool to a cohort of trainings across a variety of EBPs. Pilot testing of the tool is needed to evaluate the *usability* of the tool. Specifically, pilot testing will inform refinements needed to improve clarity in the concepts and language, ease of rating (e.g., distinguishing between a 2 and a 3), availability of training information necessary to assign ratings, and ease of scoring. This pilot testing will also allow evaluation of the *validity* of the tool. Specifically, by applying the tool to trainings with a range of stated training goals (e.g., from raising awareness to building competence), the tool can be evaluated to assess its ability to distinguish between trainings.

In addition, the *utility* of the TIP Tool results should be evaluated and refined across various stakeholders. For example, it will be essential to demonstrate that training leaders/organizations find the results useful and that the results provide ideas for specific changes if a training's leader/organization would like to shift from the Raising Awareness level to the Skill-Building level. Feedback from other stakeholders, such as organizations and clinicians interested in understanding more about training options, will also be important to assess.

Finally, it will be necessary to ensure the *reliability* of the tool. To examine interrater reliability, pilot testing should involve multiple independent raters using the same information about the training. An assessor training plan may be needed to ensure that external assessors are able to apply the tool consistently. Training leaders/organizations may choose to self-assess; it would be useful to determine whether self-assessments produce scores that are higher than assessments conducted by external, objective assessors. These additional development and refinement steps will ensure that the TIP Tool meets its objectives for a variety of stakeholders and users.

Recommendations to Improve Training of the Mental Health Workforce in Delivering Evidence-Based Psychotherapies

It is essential to ensure that the mental health workforce is trained to meet the mental health needs of the communities it serves. Research has demonstrated that there are specific EBPs that can be used to accelerate symptom reduction and recovery. Thus, to ensure that those with mental health conditions achieve recovery, they must have access to EBPs. This requires that the mental health workforce is well-educated, equipped, and ready to deliver evidence-based approaches for specific mental health conditions. A key component of preparing the mental health workforce is training. As such, ensuring that the mental health workforce is trained in a manner that has a higher likelihood of facilitating its competency in and use of EBPs becomes critical. Below we outline several recommendations for improving training of the mental health workforce for delivering EBPs.

Implement Independent Assessments of Training Programs

There is a need for increased focus on improving the quality of psychotherapy training for clinicians who are already practicing. Typically, each licensed clinician is required to complete a minimum number of continuing education credits during each licensure renewal period. However, it is unclear whether or how the continuing education credit accrual alone might ensure the achievement of proficiency or competency in specific EBPs. Given the significant variability in the types of trainings offered to licensed clinicians, encouraging additional independent assessments of these programs could help to assess the likelihood of these different types of trainings facilitating competency and adoption of EBPs.

Incorporate New Requirements into Licensure and Certification Exams

Another approach to ensuring accountability in achieving competency in EBPs might be to incorporate new requirements into the licensure and certification requirements for the mental health workforce. There are certain challenges to incorporating these new requirements into existing licensure requirements. For one, licensure requirements vary from state to state and by profession (e.g., social workers and clinical psychologists might have different requirements to renew licensure). In addition, not all mental health providers work in a capacity in which they provide therapy (e.g., neuropsychologists). However, there may still be opportunities to require practicing clinicians to demonstrate competency in EBPs for certain certifications. For example, there is an increasing movement toward board certification among clinical psychologists. Though certification is not required for practice, the American Board of Professional Psychology certifies clinicians who have achieved competence in a given specialty area (American Board of Professional Psychology, undated[c]). Some of these subspecialties are geared toward clinicians who provide psychotherapy, such as clinical psychology, for which intervention is a core competency (American Board of Professional Psychology, undated[a]). To become certified by the American Board of Professional Psychology, a psychologist must submit two video-recorded work samples (American Board of Professional Psychology, undated[b]); however, there is no requirement that these work samples reflect an EBP. Incorporating this type of requirement would allow clinicians the flexibility to select the specific EBP that is relevant to the patient population that they serve while still ensuring that board-certified clinicians have demonstrated competency with at least one EBP.

Offer New Standardized Certification Opportunities

Another approach to ensuring accountability in achieving competency in EBPs might be to create additional standardized opportunities for certification for the mental health workforce. For example, the Academy of Cognitive Therapy awards certification to clinicians who demonstrate expertise in cognitive therapy. To be eligible for certification, clinicians must meet certain requirements related to education in cognitive therapy and clinical experience. In addition, each clinician must demonstrate clinical competency in cognitive therapy, which is evaluated through the submission of a case sample, including an audio recording of a treatment session (Academy of Cognitive Therapy, undated). Though some trainings may offer informal certification opportunities, creating more opportunities for formal certification through the demonstration of clinical competency may be one way to ensure a well-trained workforce.

Ultimately, these improvements in the training of the mental health workforce have important implications for patient outcomes. EBPs often emphasize measurement-based care—the administration of symptom measures over time to inform clinical decisionmaking at the individual patient level (Fortney et al., 2016). Not only does this allow clinicians the opportunity to adjust the course of care to better adapt to the specific needs of the patient, but research has also demonstrated that measurement-based care has a positive effect on patient outcomes (Fortney et al., 2016). In this way, providing high-quality training to the mental health workforce will ensure that patients have access to the most-effective available treatments, delivered in a way that meets their individual needs.

APPENDIX A

Development of the Tool

To inform the development of this tool to assess psychotherapy trainings, we conducted a comprehensive review of the peer-reviewed literature on trainings for evidence-based therapies to treat MDD, PTSD, and SUD. We sought to identify common themes among successful psychotherapy trainings, and we focused on measures of treatment fidelity—or psychotherapy adherence and competence—as the primary indicators of the success of a training (Perepletchikova and Kazdin, 2005).

Scope of Search and Discussions

Diagnoses of Focus

We focused on trainings that taught clinicians to deliver at least one evidence-based psychotherapy for MDD, PTSD, or SUD. These diagnoses are among the most common for patients who receive psychotherapy in community-based settings, particularly among veterans. These are also diagnoses for which there are effective psychotherapies.

Evidence-Based Practices

We operationally defined evidence-based psychotherapy using the VA and DoD clinical practice guidelines for the management of each disorder (Management of Major Depressive Disorder Working Group, 2016; Management of Posttraumatic Stress Disorder Work Group, 2017; Management of Substance Use Disorders Work Group, 2015). We supplemented these guidelines with the American Psychological Association's *Clinical Practice Guideline for the Treatment of Posttraumatic Stress Disorder (PTSD) in Adults* (American Psychological Association, 2017) because these were the most recent guidelines for PTSD. We included only those treatments for which the evidence base was classified as "strong for" (Institute of Medicine, 2011).[1]

The list of interventions that met these criteria—the target psychotherapies—appear in Table A.1. Note that, within the SUD clinical practice guideline, interventions were identified and organized by specific SUDs (e.g., alcohol use disorder), which is reflected in the table.

Details about the literature search strategy, including the search terms, review strategy, data abstraction process, and an overview of the search results are included below. We also integrated findings from consultation with five experts. These individuals were selected based

[1] The "strong for" classification reflects the Grading of Recommendations Assessment, Development, and Evaluation (GRADE) approach to classifying recommendations in practice guidelines (Andrews et al., 2013). In the GRADE approach, recommendations are categorized according to strength (strong versus weak) and direction (for or against a given practice).

Table A.1
Evidence-Based Psychotherapies, by Diagnosis

Diagnosis	Evidence-Based Psychotherapies
MDD	• Acceptance and commitment therapy • Behavioral activation/behavioral therapy • CBT • Interpersonal psychotherapy • Mindfulness-based therapies • Problem-solving therapy
PTSD	• Prolonged exposure* • Cognitive processing therapy* • Eye movement desensitization and reprocessing • Specific CBTs for PTSD* • Brief eclectic psychotherapy • Narrative exposure therapy • Written narrative exposure
SUD	Alcohol use disorder • Behavioral couples therapy for alcohol use disorder • CBT for SUDs • Community reinforcement approach • Motivational enhancement therapy • 12-step facilitation Cannabis use disorder • CBT • Motivational enhancement therapy • Combined CBT and motivational enhancement therapy Stimulant use disorder (e.g., cocaine, methamphetamine) • CBT • General drug counseling • Community reinforcement approach

NOTE: All of the interventions for PTSD were identified in the VA/DoD guidelines;

* These interventions were also identified in the American Psychological Association PTSD guidelines.

on their publication track records and national recognition as experts in the development of and training in specific psychotherapies, psychotherapy training, and implementation science. We also sought feedback from seven experts on early drafts of the TIP Tool to ensure that items were written clearly, with sufficient scoring guidance, and that items adequately reflected the core elements of effective psychotherapy trainings. Selected experts participated in both activities.

The purpose of these discussions was to gather expert feedback and insights on what these leaders perceived as the characteristics and components of trainings that contributed to provider competency. Most of these individuals had designed, evaluated, and refined psychotherapy trainings. Experts were drawn from multiple settings, including academia and training organizations.

Search Strategy

Search Parameters

To determine the evidence for practitioner trainings on evidence-based psychotherapies for MDD, PTSD, and SUD, we conducted a search of the peer-reviewed literature. The searches were conducted in November and December 2017 using three databases: PsycINFO, Published International Literature on Traumatic Stress (PILOTS), and PubMed. We limited our search results to English-language, peer-reviewed literature published from 1992 to 2017, inclusive. We used a broad definition of *training* for this search, ranging from one-time courses or workshops to formal, ongoing trainings, and we did not restrict our search by treatment setting.

To ensure that we captured all relevant articles, we supplemented our search by reviewing articles that cited a seminal article (Sholomskas, Syracuse-Siewert, et al., 2005) that evaluated the effectiveness of various methods for training clinicians to implement evidence-based psychotherapy. The search was conducted in December 2017 using two databases: Scopus and Web of Science. We limited our search results to English-language, peer-reviewed literature published from 2005 to 2017, inclusive. We included any articles that cited Sholomskas, Syracuse-Siewert, et al. (2005) for this search, and we did not restrict by treatment setting, evidence-based practice, or diagnosis.

Search Terms

Search terms were developed to represent the key objectives, including training-related terms, diagnosis- and evidence-based psychotherapy-related terms, and evaluation terms. We conducted an initial pilot test of these terms and then refined the strategy prior to conducting a final search. We conducted separate searches for each diagnostic category, customizing to the database searched. Each search statement was created by combining training-related terms, such as "curriculum," "continuing education," or "workshop," with evaluation-related terms, such as "dissemination" or "fidelity," and terms to capture diagnostic category and EBP type. We searched title, abstract, and/or subject fields in PsycINFO and PILOTS and created separate search terms for title or abstract and Medical Subject Headings (MeSH) in PubMed. Exact search statements are provided in Appendix B.

Review Process

The search yielded 1,517 records (e.g., articles, book chapters) identified through our search terms and 400 records that cited Sholomskas et al. (2005) (see Figure A.1). After removing duplicates, there were 1,845 unique records. A preliminary screen was done by reviewing the titles and abstracts to determine the relevance of each record and to eliminate any non–peer-reviewed literature (e.g., book chapters) that was inadvertently captured in the search results. This preliminary screen of unique records was followed by a full-text review of relevant peer-reviewed articles.

To limit the scope of our review, we focused on articles providing descriptions and evaluations of trainings, as well as articles that described trainings that were offered within the context of treatment trials (e.g., therapy training provided to research study clinicians). We included psychotherapy trainings conducted in military, veteran, and civilian behavioral health settings and focused on trainings for providers serving adult patients.

Of the 1,845 unique records that were identified, the majority (n = 1,559) were excluded. Many of these records described trainings on therapy types not included in our list of target psychotherapies (Table A.1), or they were treatment efficacy trials with no training component. We also excluded training-themed articles that discussed psychotherapy training broadly with no description of a particular training and general articles about training on diagnostics, clini-

Figure A.1
Literature Search Flow Diagram

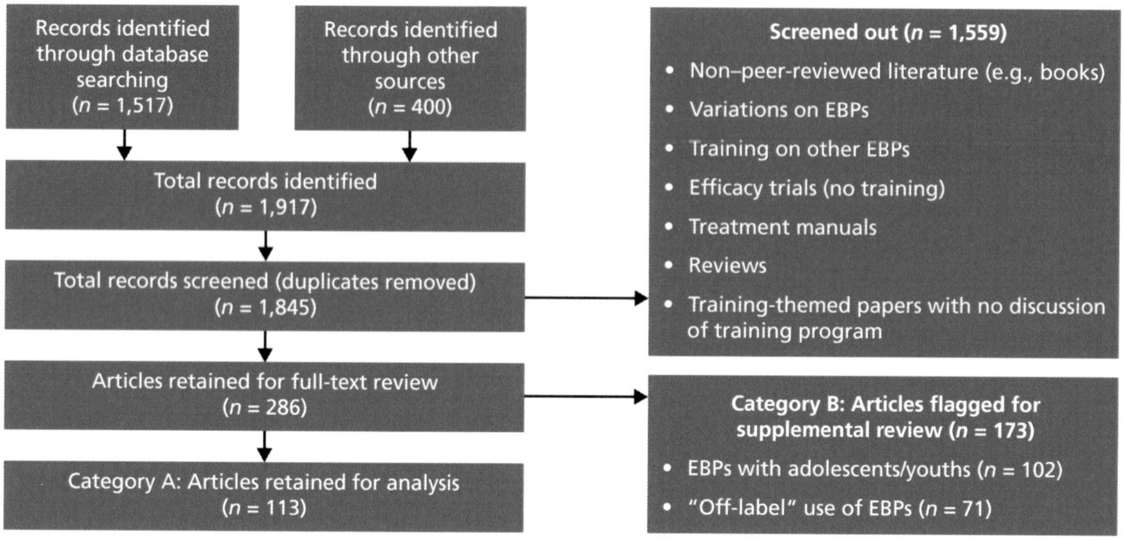

RAND *TL306-A.1*

cal case formulation, and psychotherapy ethics. Systematic reviews and other qualitative review articles were excluded, though reviews of trainings that were inclusive of the target psychotherapies and diagnoses were examined to screen bibliographies for additional sources of relevant peer-reviewed literature. As stated above, we excluded any non–peer-reviewed literature (e.g., book chapters). No additional articles were identified through this supplemental examination of literature review bibliographies.

There were 286 articles that met our criteria for inclusion and focused on the EBPs of interest. Of these, 113 articles pertained to our target psychotherapies and diagnoses in adult populations. Because our focus was on adult populations, these articles were classified as Category A. This category also included articles in which the diagnosis of focus was not specified explicitly in the text but in which the clinical population was consistent with the diagnoses of interest, as well as articles describing trainings that were explicitly transdiagnostic and included at least one of the diagnoses of interest. Therefore, all articles made some explicit mention of one of our three target diagnoses (MDD, PTSD, or SUD) in reference to the patient population, the target diagnosis of the psychotherapy training, or both. Articles about trainings that focused on co-occurring MDD, PTSD, and/or SUD were also coded and retained in Category A.

In addition, 71 articles described trainings that utilized one of the target psychotherapies for a treatment indication other than MDD, PTSD, or SUD—such as schizophrenia or chronic pain—and 102 articles described trainings that utilized one of the target psychotherapies with child or adolescent populations. These articles were classified as Category B. We flagged these 173 articles to be considered during a separate stage of analysis.

Data Abstraction

Our primary focus in the data abstraction process was on Category A articles. A coding sheet was created, and data were abstracted for each full-text article in the following categories:

- study methodology
- focus of the training (e.g., diagnosis, EBP, population of focus)
- training characteristics, including training timing, length, and level of interactivity (e.g., didactic, interactive, and experiential elements)
- consultation or supervision characteristics (e.g., format, use of session review)
- nature of the training evaluation, including type of process or outcome measure (e.g., adherence, competence, pre/post knowledge and skills testing, satisfaction, patient outcomes) and results of the evaluation.

A team of three coders completed the abstraction process; though each article was coded by only one coder, we frequently discussed coding decisions and challenging articles to ensure consistency in coding. Free-text fields were utilized to capture additional details during abstraction for fields that were more varied or challenging to characterize with a singular coding response (e.g., level of interactivity).

We supplemented this detailed abstraction of Category A articles with a review of Category B and review articles. Regarding review articles, we focused on the articles that were flagged during our initial screening to identify any conclusions about training elements deemed most important for bringing clinicians to adherence and competence in delivering the target psychotherapy. Though not all the studies included in these review articles were focused on our diagnoses or EBPs of interest, these findings were used to determine whether the results of our primary abstraction and analysis were consistent with findings from the broader literature. We recorded any findings regarding effective training elements, as well as limitations of the literature that were highlighted in the reviews.

In addition, we examined a subset of the Category B articles, focusing on the most methodologically rigorous articles: RCTs of trainings, specifically those that assessed for adherence or competence. Of the 173 Category B articles, we identified seven RCTs of training programs, of which four assessed competence or adherence. We abstracted the key findings of these studies, synthesizing across the different trainings and articles to identify common themes. These were used to supplement the review of Category A articles.

Results

As described, 113 unique articles were included in Category A. Of these, 22 described more than one training (e.g., studies describing different methods of training providers to deliver a given intervention). The most commonly reported diagnosis of focus was MDD (39 percent), followed by PTSD (24 percent) and SUD (17 percent) (see Figure A.2).

Training Characteristics

A total of 137 trainings were described across the 113 articles because several articles compared different EBP trainings for the same clinical population (with contrasting training elements

Figure A.2
Target Diagnoses of Psychotherapy Training (*N* = 113)

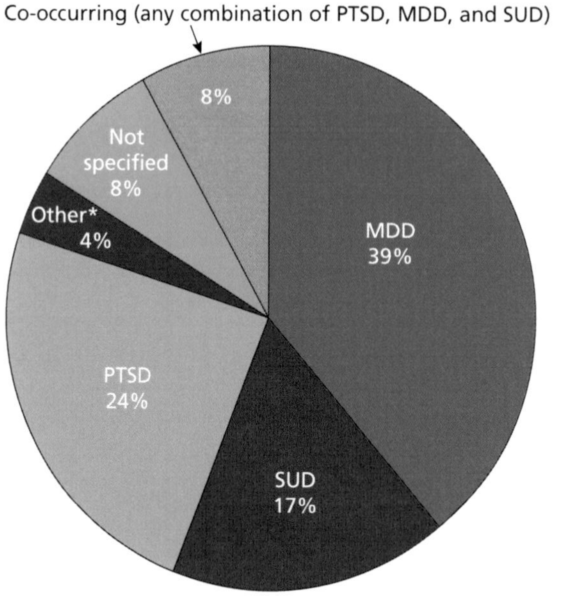

NOTE: Each of the 113 unique articles is counted only once.
* The "other" category includes studies that focused on multiple conditions (with one condition being one of the target diagnoses [PTSD, MDD, or SUD]) and transdiagnostic studies.
RAND *TL306-A.2*

or patient outcomes) or examined trainings for two types of EBPs for the same diagnosis. CBT was the reported focus of most of the literature that we reviewed; 75 (55 percent) of the 137 trainings were CBT focused (Table A.2). Behavioral activation/behavioral therapy, cognitive processing therapy, and prolonged exposure were the next–most-represented EBPs in this subset of the literature, but less than 10 percent of the articles focused on each of these treatments.

Descriptions of trainings reported in the literature were highly variable with respect to timing (whether they were spaced over time or delivered as a massed workshop over one or multiple days), format (self-guided, trainer led, or computer assisted), and content (didactic, interactive, or experiential), even within the same treatment modality. The literature was also varied in the degree of detail provided about training and supervision.

Supervision was reported in the majority (80 percent) of trainings. Of those articles that described trainings with supervision, over half (59 percent) were conducted in a group format. Session review was reported in just over half (57 percent) of all articles. Of those articles that described trainings with session review, 40 (64 percent) reported utilizing audio session review, 16 (25 percent) video, 12 (19 percent) clinician report of the session, seven (11 percent) a combination of audio and video, and three (5 percent) live viewing of the session.

Of the 113 unique articles, 106 (94 percent) reported the results of some sort of evaluation, including both process (e.g., participant satisfaction) and outcome measures. A subset of articles (n = 7; 6 percent) were protocol descriptions or otherwise did not report outcomes. There was great variability in the study methodology utilized across the 106 articles that reported the results of an evaluation, including 15 training RCTs (14 percent), 22 treatment

Table A.2
Type of Psychotherapy Training (*N* = 137)

Therapy	Number	Percentage
Behavioral activation/behavioral therapy	11	8%
CBT	75	55%
Cognitive processing therapy	10	7%
Interpersonal therapy	7	5%
Prolonged exposure	10	7%
Other[a]	24	18%
Total	137	100%

NOTE: This table reflects data for 137 trainings described in 113 unique articles.

[a] "Other" includes acceptance and commitment therapy (1.5 percent), behavioral couples therapy for alcohol use disorder (0.7 percent), combined CBT and motivational enhancement therapy (1.5 percent), eye movement desensitization and reprocessing (0.7 percent), general drug counseling (1.5 percent), mindfulness-based therapies (2.2 percent), motivational enhancement therapy (2.9 percent), narrative exposure therapy (2.2 percent), problem-solving therapy (2.2 percent), community reinforcement (0.7 percent), CBT using brief imaginal exposure (0.7 percent), and 12-step facilitation (0.7 percent).

RCTs that described a training component (21 percent), and 69 other methodologies (65 percent), such as pre/post, cross-sectional/observational, and mixed methods. Articles described trainings that utilized many different measures to assess outcomes, including standardized tools (e.g., validated scales to assess adherence, competence, or knowledge), clinician self-report (e.g., skills utilization, perceived self-efficacy, knowledge, attitudes/beliefs), and unvalidated questionnaires (e.g., fidelity assessments or questionnaires about barriers to implementation that were developed for the particular training or treatment trial). Many articles described trainings that evaluated patient outcomes—especially in the case of treatment RCTs—but, in most cases, there was no analysis to determine whether training-related variables contributed to these outcomes. Frequencies of different evaluation outcomes utilized across trainings are summarized in Figure A.3.

Figure A.3
Type of Evaluation for Trainings (*N* = 137)

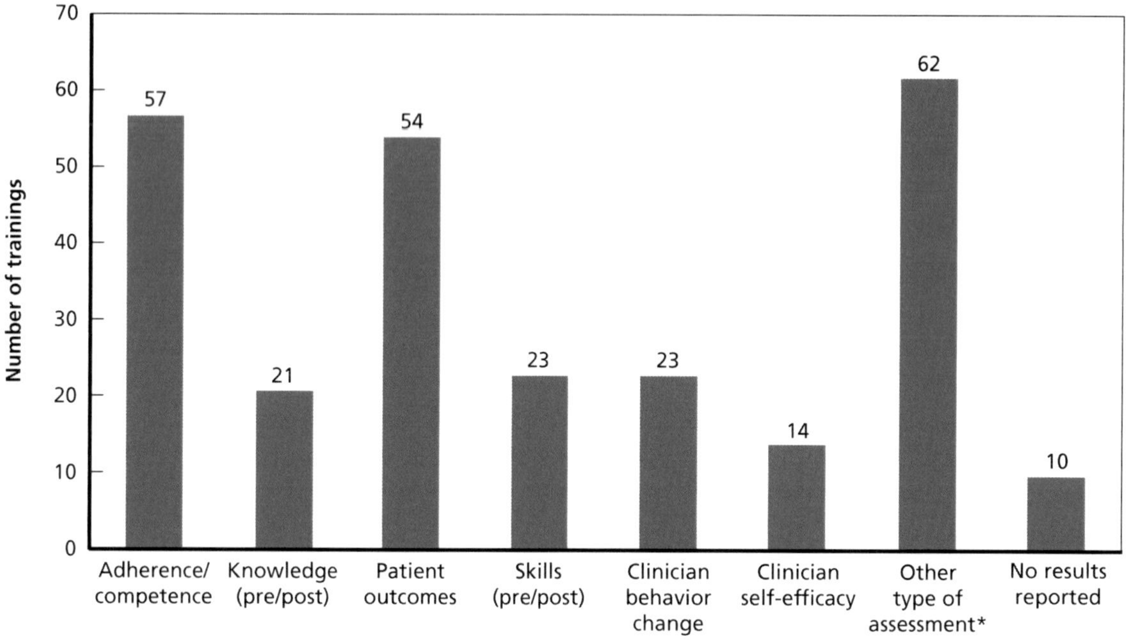

NOTE: There were 137 trainings described in 113 articles. Seven of these 113 articles, which described ten of the 137 trainings, did not report any results of an evaluation.
* Examples of other types of assessment include measures of clinician attitudes, clinician-identified barriers to implementation, job burnout, therapeutic alliance, patient motivation, and patient satisfaction.
RAND *TL306-A.3*

APPENDIX B

Search Statements

PsycINFO: Searching in the Title, Abstract, and Subject Fields, Unless Otherwise Noted

Depression

(["psychotherapy training" OR "clinical methods training" OR training OR "training program*" OR "professional training" OR "didactic training" OR "continuing education" OR workshop*] OR [search in title or subject fields][curriculum OR instruct* OR seminar* OR class OR classes OR educat*])

AND

("major depression" OR depression OR MDD)

AND

("acceptance and commitment therapy" OR "acceptance therapy" OR "acceptance based therapy" OR "behavi* therapy" OR "behavi* activation" OR "cognitive behavi* therapy" OR CBT OR "interpersonal therapy" OR IPT OR "mindfulness based cognitive therapy" OR "problem solving therapy")

AND

(adher* OR fidelity OR competence OR "professional competence" OR "professional development" OR certif* OR evaluat* OR "program evaluation" OR implement* OR disseminat*)

Posttraumatic Stress Disorder

(["psychotherapy training" OR "clinical methods training" OR training OR "training program*" OR "professional training" OR "didactic training" OR "continuing education" OR workshop*] OR [search in title or subject fields][curriculum OR instruct* OR seminar* OR class OR classes OR educat*])

AND

("posttraumatic stress disorder" OR "post traumatic stress" OR trauma OR PTSD)

AND

("prolonged exposure" OR "cognitive processing therapy" OR CPT OR "eye movement desensitization and reprocessing" OR EMDR OR "cognitive behavi* therapy" OR CBT OR "brief eclectic psychotherapy" OR "BEP-TG" OR "narrative exposure therapy" OR "written narrative exposure")

AND

(adher* OR fidelity OR competence OR "professional competence" OR "professional development" OR certif* OR evaluat* OR "program evaluation" OR implement* OR disseminat*)

Substance Use Disorder

(["psychotherapy training" OR "clinical methods training" OR training OR "training program*" OR "professional training" OR "didactic training" OR "continuing education" OR workshop*] OR [search in title or subject fields][curriculum OR instruct* OR seminar* OR class OR classes OR educat*])

AND

("substance abuse disorder*" OR SUD OR AUD OR "alcohol abuse" OR alcoholism OR "drug abuse" OR "drug dependency" OR "drug addiction" OR addiction OR "substance use disorder*")

AND

("behavi* couples therapy" OR "cognitive behavi* therapy" OR CBT OR "community reinforcement approach" OR "motivational enhancement therapy" OR "12-step facilitation" OR TSF)

AND

(adher* OR fidelity OR competence OR "professional competence" OR "professional development" OR certif* OR evaluat* OR "program evaluation" OR implement* OR disseminat*)

PILOTS: Searching in the Title, Abstract, and Subject Fields, Unless Otherwise Noted

Depression

(["psychotherapy training" OR "clinical methods training" OR training OR "training program*" OR "professional training" OR "didactic training" OR "continuing education" OR workshop*] OR [search in title or subject fields][curriculum OR instruct* OR seminar* OR class OR classes OR educat*])

AND

("major depression" OR depression OR "depressive disorders" OR MDD)

AND

("acceptance and commitment therapy" OR "acceptance therapy" OR "acceptance based therapy" OR "behavi* therapy" OR "behavi* activation" OR "cognitive behavi* therapy" OR CBT OR "interpersonal therapy" OR IPT OR "mindfulness based cognitive therapy" OR "problem solving therapy")

AND

(adher* OR fidelity OR competence OR "professional competence" OR "professional development" OR certif* OR evaluat* OR "program evaluation" OR implement* OR disseminat*)

Posttraumatic Stress Disorder

(["psychotherapy training" OR "clinical methods training" OR training OR "training program*" OR "professional training" OR "didactic training" OR "continuing education" OR workshop*] OR [search in title or subject fields][curriculum OR instruct* OR seminar* OR class OR classes OR educat*])

AND

("posttraumatic stress disorder" OR "post traumatic stress" OR trauma OR PTSD)

AND

("prolonged exposure" OR "cognitive processing therapy" OR CPT OR "eye movement desensitization and reprocessing" OR EMDR OR "cognitive behavi* therapy" OR CBT OR "brief eclectic psychotherapy" OR "BEP-TG" OR "narrative exposure therapy" OR "written narrative exposure")

AND

(adher* OR fidelity OR competence OR "professional competence" OR "professional development" OR certif* OR evaluat* OR "program evaluation" OR implement* OR disseminat*)

Substance Use Disorder

(["psychotherapy training" OR "clinical methods training" OR training OR "training program*" OR "professional training" OR "didactic training" OR "continuing education" OR workshop*] OR [search in title or subject fields][curriculum OR instruct* OR seminar* OR class OR classes OR educat*])

AND

("substance abuse disorder*" OR SUD OR AUD OR "alcohol abuse" OR alcoholism OR "drug abuse" OR "drug dependency" OR "drug addiction" OR addiction OR "substance use disorder*")

AND

("behavi* couples therapy" OR "cognitive behavi* therapy" OR CBT OR "community reinforcement approach" OR "motivational enhancement therapy" OR "12-step facilitation" OR TSF)

AND

(adher* OR fidelity OR competence OR "professional competence" OR "professional development" OR certif* OR evaluat* OR "program evaluation" OR implement* OR disseminat*)

PubMed: Searching as noted in [tiab] = title or abstract, [ti] = title, and [mh] = Medical Subject Headings (including all terms below in the hierarchy)

Depression

(psychotherapy train*[tiab] OR clinical methods train*[tiab] OR train[tiab] OR training[tiab] OR training program*[tiab] OR professional train*[tiab] OR curriculum[ti] OR curriculum[mh] OR instruct[ti] OR instructing[ti] OR instruction[ti] OR seminar*[ti] OR class[ti] OR classes[ti] OR educat*[ti] OR education[mh] OR continuing education[tiab] OR didactic training[tiab] OR workshop*[tiab])

AND

(major depression*[tiab] OR depression*[tiab] OR MDD[tiab] OR depression[mh])

AND

(acceptance and commitment therapy[tiab] OR acceptance and commitment therapy[mh] OR acceptance therapy[tiab] OR acceptance based therapy[tiab] OR behavior therapy[tiab] OR behaviour therapy[tiab] OR behavior therapy[mh] OR behavior activation[tiab] OR behaviour activation[tiab] OR cognitive behavior therapy[tiab] OR cognitive behaviour therapy[tiab] OR CBT[tiab] OR cognitive behavioral therapy[tiab] OR cognitive behavioural therapy[tiab] OR cognitive therapy[mh] OR interpersonal therapy[tiab] OR IPT[tiab] OR mindfulness based cognitive therapy[tiab] OR problem solving therapy[tiab])

AND

(adherence[tiab] OR guideline adherence[mh] OR fidelity[tiab] OR competence[tiab] OR professional competence[tiab] OR professional competence[mh] OR professional development[tiab] OR certification[tiab] OR certifying[tiab] OR certification[mh] OR evaluat*[tiab] OR program evaluation[tiab] OR program evaluation[mh] OR information dissemination[mh] OR disseminat*[tiab] OR implement*[tiab])

Posttraumatic Stress Disorder

(psychotherapy train*[tiab] OR clinical methods train*[tiab] OR train[tiab] OR training[tiab] OR training program*[tiab] OR professional train*[tiab] OR curriculum[ti] OR curriculum[mh] OR instruct[ti] OR instructing[ti] OR instruction[ti] OR seminar*[ti] OR class[ti] OR classes[ti] OR educat*[ti] OR education[mh] OR continuing education[tiab] OR didactic training[tiab] OR workshop*[tiab])

AND

(ptsd[tiab] OR stress disorders, post-traumatic[mh] OR posttraumatic stress disorder*[tiab] OR post traumatic stress disorder*[tiab] OR psychological trauma[mh])

AND

(prolonged exposure[tiab] OR implosive therapy[mh] OR cognitive processing therapy[tiab] OR CPT[tiab] OR eye movement desensitization and reprocessing [tiab] OR EMDR[tiab] OR eye movement desensitization reprocessing[mh] OR cognitive behavioral therapy[tiab] OR cognitive behavioural therapy[tiab] OR cognitive behavior therapy[tiab] OR cognitive behaviour therapy[tiab] OR cognitive therapy[mh] OR CBT[tiab] OR brief eclectic psychotherapy[tiab] OR BEP-TG[tiab] OR narrative exposure therapy[tiab] OR written narrative exposure[tiab])

AND

(adherence[tiab] OR guideline adherence[mh] OR fidelity[tiab] OR competence[tiab] OR professional competence[tiab] OR professional competence[mh] OR professional development[tiab] OR certification[tiab] OR certifying[tiab] OR certification[mh] OR evaluat*[tiab] OR program evaluation[tiab] OR program evaluation[mh] OR information dissemination[mh] OR disseminat*[tiab] OR implement*[tiab])

Substance Use Disorder

(psychotherapy train*[tiab] OR clinical methods train*[tiab] OR train[tiab] OR training[tiab] OR training program*[tiab] OR professional train*[tiab] OR curriculum[ti] OR curriculum[mh] OR instruct[ti] OR instructing[ti] OR instruction[ti] OR seminar*[ti] OR class[ti] OR classes[ti] OR educat*[ti] OR education[mh] OR continuing education[tiab] OR didactic training[tiab] OR workshop*[tiab])

AND

(substance-related disorders[mh] OR substance use disorder*[tiab] OR AUD[tiab] OR SUD[tiab] OR alcohol abuse[tiab] OR alcoholism[tiab] OR drug abuse[tiab] OR drug dependency[tiab] OR drug addiction*[tiab] OR addiction[tiab])

AND

(cognitive behavioral therapy[tiab] OR cognitive behavioural therapy[tiab] OR cognitive behavior therapy[tiab] OR cognitive behaviour therapy[tiab] OR cognitive therapy[mh] OR CBT[tiab] OR behavioral couples therapy[tiab] OR behavioural couples therapy[tiab] OR community reinforcement approach[tiab] OR motivational enhancement therapy[tiab] or 12 step facilitation[tiab])

AND

(adherence[tiab] OR guideline adherence[mh] OR fidelity[tiab] OR competence[tiab] OR professional competence[tiab] OR professional competence[mh] OR professional development[tiab] OR certification[tiab] OR certifying[tiab] OR certification[mh] OR evaluat*[tiab] OR program evaluation[tiab] OR program evaluation[mh] OR information dissemination[mh] OR disseminat*[tiab] OR implement*[tiab])

APPENDIX C

The TIP Tool

Training in Psychotherapy (TIP) Tool: Training Program Identification

Date __________ **Raters** ______________________________

Training Name ______________________________

Website ______________________________

Address ______________________________

Program Contact ______________________________

Telephone Number ______________________________

Email Address ______________________________

Training Characteristics

Target Psychotherapies Addressed by Training

____

____

____

____

____

Target Diagnoses Addressed by Training

____

____

____

____

____

Training Size

Number of trainings per year: __________

Average number of trainees per training: __________

Training Format

In person: ☐ Available ☐ Required

Web based: ☐ Available ☐ Required

Minimum Qualification of Trainees

____

____

____

____

____

____

Typical Length of Didactic Training

__________ hours

Typical Timing of Didactic Training

☐ One time, consecutive days
☐ Spaced out over time

Training in Psychotherapy (TIP) Tool: Scored Domains

	1 = Raising Awareness	2	3 = Skill-Building	4	5 = Supporting Competence
I. Didactic Training Format					
IA. Length of Training	2 hours or less	3 to 5 hours	6 to 8 hours	9 to 15 hours	16+ hours
IB. Level of Interactivity	Self-guided	**Didactic** only	Didactic, plus *either* **demonstrations** or **other interactive elements**	Didactic, plus *both* demonstrations and other interactive elements	Didactic, plus *all* of the following: demonstrations, other interactive elements, and **role plays**
IC. Individual Feedback During Training	**Self-guided or self-generated** feedback only	Few trainees receive **informal** feedback from leader *or* peer(s)	Some but not all trainees receive informal feedback from leader *or* peer(s)	All trainees receive informal feedback from leader *or* peer(s)	**Structured**, individual feedback
ID. Integration of Written Materials	No use of **written materials**	Written materials provided but not integrated into didactic training	Review of written materials suggested before or after didactic training	Review of written materials strongly encouraged but not required	Review of written materials required before or after didactic training
II. Didactic Training Content					
IIA. Core Techniques and Theory	Not included	Concepts addressed in **supplemental materials** or resources but not discussed in didactic training	Concepts introduced in didactic training	Concepts discussed with examples in didactic training	Trainees given opportunity to practice or apply concepts in didactic training
IIB. Clinical Judgment and Decisionmaking	Not included	Concepts addressed in supplemental materials or resources but not discussed in didactic training	Concepts introduced in didactic training	Concepts discussed with examples in didactic training	Trainees given opportunity to practice or apply concepts in didactic training
IIC. Addressing Co-Occurring Disorders	Not included	Concept addressed in supplemental materials or resources but not discussed in didactic training	Concept introduced in didactic training	Concept discussed with examples in didactic training	Trainees given opportunity to practice or apply concept in didactic training
IID. Measurement-Based Care	Not included	Concept addressed in supplemental materials or resources but not discussed in didactic training	Concept introduced in didactic training	Concept discussed with examples in didactic training	Trainees given opportunity to practice or apply concept in didactic training

	1 = Raising Awareness	2	3 = Skill-Building	4	5 = Supporting Competence
III. Consultation/Supervision					
IIIA. Availability of Consultation/ Supervision	Not referenced	Consultation/ supervision (from training or training partner) is referenced during didactic training	Consultation/ supervision (from training or training partner) is available and is suggested	Consultation/ supervision (from training or training partner) is available and is encouraged	Consultation/ supervision (from training or training partner) is available and is required
IIIB. Review of Sessions	Not available	Formal review of **trainee therapy sessions** is not provided but is suggested	Written or spoken self-report of trainee therapy session(s) reviewed	Live or recorded trainee therapy session(s) reviewed and evaluated without a structured coding tool	Live or recorded therapy session(s) reviewed and evaluated using a structured coding tool
IIIC. Supervision Length	No consultation/ supervision provided	Consultation/ supervision provided, but no specified length or case target	Consultation/ supervision provided for at least two months	Consultation/ supervision provided for at least six months or until trainee demonstrates adherence and competence with one patient	Consultation/ supervision provided and continues until trainee demonstrates adherence and competence in session with at least two patients
IIID. Certification	Training does not mention **certification** to trainees	Supplemental materials or resources mention certification but not discussed in didactic training	Certification is mentioned during training or supervision as an option	Certification is encouraged	Certification is strongly encouraged and training tracks number of trainees who receive certification
IV. Program Evaluation					
IVA. Course Evaluation	No course evaluation of the training	Optional course evaluation or other opportunity to share trainee feedback with the training	Required assessment of trainee experience with the training	Information from the required assessment of trainee experience with the training is routinely shared with trainers	Information from the required assessment of trainee experience with training is used to improve training content, format, and facilitation
IVB. Knowledge	No assessment of trainee knowledge	Brief post-training assessment (5 items or fewer) of **trainee-perceived knowledge** change	Post-training assessment of trainee-perceived knowledge change	Post-training **test** of trainee knowledge	Pre- and post-training test of trainee knowledge
IVC. Skills	No assessment of trainee skills	Post-training assessment of trainee-perceived skills	Post-training assessment of trainee-perceived ability to use specific skills	Post-training assessment of trainee self-reported confidence in applying specific skills	Post-training assessment of trainee ability to use specific skills (e.g., role play)

	1 = Raising Awareness	2	3 = Skill-Building	4	5 = Supporting Competence
V. Implementation Facilitation					
VA. Development of an Implementation Plan	Not present	Course materials or didactic training references indicate that trainees should consider developing a plan for implementation	Course materials or didactic training describes how to develop a plan for implementation	Training provides time for clinicians to develop a basic plan for implementation	Training includes the development of a comprehensive plan for implementation
VB. Assessment of Organizational Context	Not present	Course materials or didactic training indicates that organizational context should be considered	Course materials or didactic training describes how to assess organizational context, including potential barriers to implementation	Course materials or didactic training provides specific suggestions for overcoming implementation barriers	Training includes a structured assessment plan to identify potential barriers and solutions at trainee's site
VC. Implementation Support	Not available	Implementation support is not available, but self-guided use of **outside resources** is suggested	Brief implementation consultation is available from training	Implementation support is available from the training	Full implementation support is available from training before and after didactic training

TIP Tool Scoring

I. Didactic Training Format

A. __________

B. __________

C. __________

D. __________

Sum (A + B + C + D): __________

Score (Sum/4): __________

☐ Raising Awareness (1.00–2.33)
☐ Skill-Building (2.34–3.66)
☐ Supporting Competence (3.67–5.00)

II. Didactic Training Content

A. __________

B. __________

C. __________

D. __________

Sum (A + B + C + D): __________

Score (Sum/4): __________

☐ Raising Awareness (1.00–2.33)
☐ Skill-Building (2.34–3.66)
☐ Supporting Competence (3.67–5.00)

III. Consultation/Supervision

A. __________

B. __________

C. __________

D. __________

Sum (A + B + C + D): __________

Score (Sum/4): __________

☐ Raising Awareness (1.00–2.33)
☐ Skill-Building (2.34–3.66)
☐ Supporting Competence (3.67–5.00)

IV. Program Evaluation

A. __________

B. __________

C. __________

Sum (A + B + C): __________

Score (Sum/3): __________

☐ Raising Awareness (1.00–2.33)
☐ Skill-Building (2.34–3.66)
☐ Supporting Competence (3.67–5.00)

V. Implementation Facilitation

A. __________

B. __________

C. __________

Sum (A + B + C): __________

Score (Sum/3): __________

☐ Raising Awareness (1.00–2.33)
☐ Skill-Building (2.34–3.66)
☐ Supporting Competence (3.67–5.00)

Training Total Score

Total sum (Items IA–VC): __________

Total score (Total sum/18): __________

☐ Raising Awareness (1.00–2.33)
☐ Skill-Building (2.34–3.66)
☐ Supporting Competence (3.67–5.00)

TIP Tool Scores

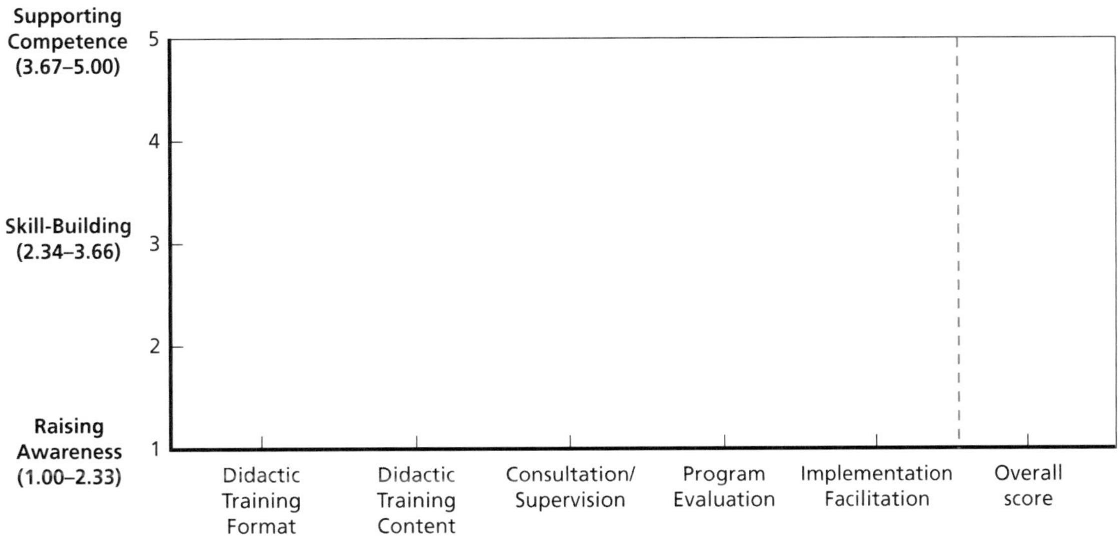

References

Academy of Cognitive Therapy, "Certification Process," undated. As of July 16, 2018:
https://www.academyofct.org/page/CertProcess

Addis, Michael E., Wendy A. Wade, and Christina Hatgis, "Barriers to Dissemination of Evidence-Based Practices: Addressing Practitioners' Concerns About Manual-Based Psychotherapies," *Clinical Psychology: Science and Practice*, Vol. 6, No. 4, 1999, pp. 430–441.

American Board of Professional Psychology, "Clinical Psychology," undated(a). As of July 16, 2018:
https://legacy.abpp.org/i4a/pages/index.cfm?pageid=3307

American Board of Professional Psychology, "Practice Samples/Written Documents," undated(b). As of July 16, 2018:
https://abpp.org/Applicant-Information/Specialty-Boards/Clinical-Psychology/Certification-Exam-Process/Practice-Sample-Information.aspx

American Board of Professional Psychology, "What Is ABPP?" undated(c). As of July 16, 2018:
https://legacy.abpp.org/i4a/pages/index.cfm?pageid=3341

American Psychological Association, *Clinical Practice Guideline for the Treatment of Posttraumatic Stress Disorder (PTSD) in Adults*, Washington, D.C., 2017.

American Psychological Association, "APA Clinical Practice Guideline Development," 2018. As of July 6, 2018:
http://www.apa.org/about/offices/directorates/guidelines/clinical-practice.aspx

American Psychiatric Association, "Clinical Practice Guidelines," 2018. As of July 16, 2018:
https://www.psychiatry.org/psychiatrists/practice/clinical-practice-guidelines

Andrews, Jeffrey C., Holger J. Schünemann, Andrew D. Oxman, Kevin Pottie, Joerg J. Meerpohl, Pablo A. Coello, David Rind, Victor M. Montori, Juan P. Brito, Susan Norris, Mahmoud Elbarbary, Piet Post, Mona Nasser, Vijay Shukla, Roman Jaeschke, Jan Brozek, Ben Djulbegovic, and Gordon Guyatt, "GRADE Guidelines: 15. Going from Evidence to Recommendation—Determinants of a Recommendation's Direction and Strength," *Journal of Clinical Epidemiology*, Vol. 66, No. 7, 2013, pp. 726–735.

Bearman, Sarah K., John R. Weisz, Bruce F. Chorpita, Kimberly Hoagwood, Alyssa Ward, Ana M. Ugueto, and Adam Bernstein, "More Practice, Less Preach? The Role of Supervision Processes and Therapist Characteristics in EBP Implementation," *Administration and Policy in Mental Health*, Vol. 40, No. 6, 2013, pp. 518–529.

Beidas, Rinad S., and Philip C. Kendall, "Training Therapists in Evidence-Based Practice: A Critical Review of Studies from a Systems-Contextual Perspective," *Clinical Psychology (New York)*, Vol. 17, No. 1, 2010, pp. 1–30.

Brooks, Adam C., Carolyn M. Carpenedo, Jaymes Fairfax-Columbo, Nicolle T. Clements, Lois A. Benishek, Dan Knoblach, Deni Carise, and Kimberly C. Kirby, "The RoadMAP Relapse Prevention Group Counseling Toolkit: Counselor Adherence and Competence Outcomes," *Journal of Substance Abuse Treatment*, Vol. 45, No. 4, 2013, pp. 356–362.

Brown, Timothy A., Laura A. Campbell, Cassandra L. Lehman, Jessica R. Grisham, and Richard B. Mancill, "Current and Lifetime Comorbidity of the DSM-IV Anxiety and Mood Disorders in a Large Clinical Sample," *Journal of Abnormal Psychology*, Vol. 110, No. 4, 2001, pp. 585–599.

Chambless, Dianne L., "Empirically Validated Treatments—What Now?" *Applied and Preventive Psychology*, Vol. 8, No. 4, 1999, pp. 281–284.

Chu, Brian C., "Empirically Supported Training Approaches: The Who, What, and How of Disseminating Psychological Interventions," *Clinical Psychology: Science and Practice*, Vol. 15, No. 4, 2008, pp. 308–312.

Cook, Joan M., Stephanie Dinnen, James C. Coyne, Richard Thompson, Vanessa Simiola, Josef I. Ruzek, and Paula P. Schnurr, "Evaluation of an Implementation Model: A National Investigation of VA Residential Programs," *Administration and Policy in Mental Health*, Vol. 42, No. 2, 2015, pp. 147–156.

Creed, Torrey A., Courtney B. Wolk, Betsy Feinberg, Arthur C. Evans, and Aaron T. Beck, "Beyond the Label: Relationship Between Community Therapists' Self-Report of a Cognitive Behavioral Therapy Orientation and Observed Skills," *Administration and Policy in Mental Health*, Vol. 43, No. 1, 2016, pp. 36–43.

Drake, Robert E., Howard H. Goldman, H. Stephen Leff, Anthony F. Lehman, Lisa Dixon, Kim T. Mueser, and William C. Torrey, "Implementing Evidence-Based Practices in Routine Mental Health Service Settings," *Psychiatric Services*, Vol. 52, No. 2, February 2001, pp. 179–182.

Eftekhari, Afsoon, Jill J. Crowley, Josef I. Ruzek, Donn W. Garvert, Bradley E. Karlin, and Craig S. Rosen, "Training in the Implementation of Prolonged Exposure Therapy: Provider Correlates of Treatment Outcome," *Journal of Traumatic Stress*, Vol. 28, No. 1, 2015, pp. 65–68.

Eibner, Christine, Heather Krull, Kristine Brown, Matthew Cefalu, Andrew W. Mulcahy, Michael Pollard, Kanaka Shetty, David M. Adamson, Ernesto F. L. Amaral, Philip Armour, Trinidad Beleche, Olena Bogdan, Jaime L. Hastings, Kandice A. Kapinos, Amii M. Kress, Joshua Mendelsohn, Rachel Ross, Carolyn M. Rutter, Robin M. Weinick, Dulani Woods, Susan D. Hosek, and Carrie M. Farmer, *Current and Projected Characteristics and Unique Health Care Needs of the Patient Population Served by the Department of Veterans Affairs*, Santa Monica, Calif.: RAND Corporation, RR-1165/1-VA, 2015. As of August 22, 2018: https://www.rand.org/pubs/research_reports/RR1165z1.html

Ekers, David M., M. S. Dawson, and E. Bailey, "Dissemination of Behavioural Activation for Depression to Mental Health Nurses: Training Evaluation and Benchmarked Clinical Outcomes," *Journal of Psychiatric and Mental Health Nursing*, Vol. 20, No. 2, 2013, pp. 186–192.

Fairburn, Christopher G., and Zafra Cooper, "Therapist Competence, Therapy Quality, and Therapist Training," *Behaviour Research and Therapy*, Vol. 49, No. 6–7, 2011, pp. 373–378.

Fals-Stewart, William, and Gary R. Birchler, "Behavioral Couples Therapy with Alcoholic Men and Their Intimate Partners: The Comparative Effectiveness of Bachelor's- and Master's-Level Counselors," *Behavior Therapy*, Vol. 33, No. 1, 2002, pp. 123–147.

Fortney, John C., Jürgen Unützer, Glenda Wrenn, Jeffrey M. Pyne, G. Richard Smith, Michael Schoenbaum, and Henry T. Harbin, "A Tipping Point for Measurement-Based Care," *Psychiatric Services*, Vol. 68, No. 2, 2016, pp. 179–188.

Generali, Margaret M., Louisa L. Foss-Kelly, and Kelly McNamara, "Barriers to Evidence-Based Counseling Practices: A Counselor Educator Training Model," *American Association of Counselor Education and Supervision Conference*, Nashville, Tenn., 2011.

Gibbons, Carly J., Charla Nich, Karen Steinberg, Roger A. Roffman, Joanne Corvino, Thomas F. Babor, and Kathleen M. Carroll, "Treatment Process, Alliance and Outcome in Brief Versus Extended Treatments for Marijuana Dependence," *Addiction*, Vol. 105, No. 10, 2010, pp. 1799–1808.

Hepner, Kimberly A., Sarah B. Hunter, Susan M. Paddock, Annie J. Zhou, and Katherine E. Watkins, "Training Addiction Counselors to Implement CBT for Depression," *Administration and Policy in Mental Health and Mental Health Services Research*, Vol. 38, No. 4, 2011, pp. 313–323.

Herschell, Amy D., David J. Kolko, Barbara L. Baumann, and Abigail C. Davis, "The Role of Therapist Training in the Implementation of Psychosocial Treatments: A Review and Critique with Recommendations," *Clinical Psychology Review*, Vol. 30, No. 4, 2010, pp. 448–466.

Hunter, Sarah B., Katherine E. Watkins, Kimberly A. Hepner, Susan M. Paddock, Brett A. Ewing, Karen C. Osilla, and Suzanne Perry, "Treating Depression and Substance Use: A Randomized Controlled Trial," *Journal of Substance Abuse Treatment*, Vol. 43, No. 2, 2012, pp. 137–151.

Institute of Medicine, *Clinical Practice Guidelines We Can Trust*, Washington, D.C.: National Academies Press, 2011.

Jacobson, Neil S., Christopher R. Martell, and Sona Dimidjian, "Behavioral Activation Treatment for Depression: Returning to Contextual Roots," *Clinical Psychology: Science and Practice*, Vol. 8, No. 3, 2001, pp. 255–270.

James, Ian A., I.-M. Blackburn, Derek L. Milne, and F. K. Reichfelt, "Moderators of Trainee Therapists' Competence in Cognitive Therapy," *British Journal of Clinical Psychology*, Vol. 40, No. 2, 2001, pp. 131–141.

Karlin, Bradley E., Gregory K. Brown, Mickey Trockel, Darby Cunning, Antonette M. Zeiss, and C. Barr Taylor, "National Dissemination of Cognitive Behavioral Therapy for Depression in the Department of Veterans Affairs Health Care System: Therapist and Patient-Level Outcomes," *Journal of Consulting and Clinical Psychology*, Vol. 80, No. 5, 2012, pp. 707–718.

Kettlewell, Paul W., "Development, Dissemination, and Implementation of Evidence-Based Treatments: Commentary," *Clinical Psychology: Science and Practice*, Vol. 11, No. 2, 2004, pp. 190–195.

Larson, Mary Jo, Maryann Amodeo, Joseph S. LoCastro, Jordana Muroff, Lauren Smith, and Eric Gerstenberger, "Randomized Trial of Web-Based Training to Promote Counselor Use of Cognitive Behavioral Therapy Skills in Client Sessions," *Substance Abuse*, Vol. 34, No. 2, 2013, pp. 179–187.

Lau, Mark A., Greg M. Dubord, and Sagar V. Parikh, "Design and Feasibility of a New Cognitive-Behavioural Therapy Course Using a Longitudinal Interactive Format," *Canadian Journal of Psychiatry/La Revue canadienne de psychiatrie*, Vol. 49, No. 10, 2004, pp. 696–700.

Lloyd, Delyth, Anne-Laure Couineau, Katherine Hawkins, Dzenana Kartal, Reginald D. Nixon, Desmond Perry, and David Forbes, "Preliminary Outcomes of Implementing Cognitive Processing Therapy for Posttraumatic Stress Disorder Across a National Veterans' Treatment Service," *Journal of Clinical Psychiatry*, Vol. 76, No. 11, 2015, pp. e1405–e1409.

Lopez, Molly A., and Monica A. Basco, "Effectiveness of Cognitive Behavioral Therapy in Public Mental Health: Comparison to Treatment as Usual for Treatment-Resistant Depression," *Administration and Policy in Mental Health and Mental Health Services Research*, Vol. 42, No. 1, 2015, pp. 87–98.

Lu, Weili, Philip T. Yanos, Jennifer D. Gottlieb, Stephanie Marcello Duva, Steven M. Silverstein, Haiyi Xie, Stanley D. Rosenberg, and Kim T. Mueser, "Use of Fidelity Assessments to Train Clinicians in the CBT for PTSD Program for Clients with Serious Mental Illness," *Psychiatric Services*, Vol. 63, No. 8, 2012, pp. 785–792.

Management of Major Depressive Disorder Working Group, "VA/DoD Clinical Practice Guideline for the Management of Major Depressive Disorder, Version 3.0," 2016. As of November 14, 2017: https://www.healthquality.va.gov/guidelines/MH/mdd/

Management of Posttraumatic Stress Disorder Work Group, "VA/DoD Clinical Practice Guideline for the Management of Posttraumatic Stress Disorder and Acute Stress Disorder, Version 3.0," 2017. As of November 14, 2017:
https://www.healthquality.va.gov/guidelines/MH/ptsd/

Management of Substance Use Disorders Work Group, "VA/DoD Clinical Practice Guideline for the Management of Substance Use Disorders, Version 3.0," 2015. As of November 14, 2017: https://www.healthquality.va.gov/guidelines/mh/sud/

Martino, Steve, Samuel Ball, Charla Nich, Tami L. Frankforter, and Kathleen M. Carroll, "Correspondence of Motivational Enhancement Treatment Integrity Ratings Among Therapists, Supervisors, and Observers," *Psychotherapy Research*, Vol. 19, No. 2, 2009, pp. 181–193.

McHugh, R. Kathryn, and David H. Barlow, "The Dissemination and Implementation of Evidence-Based Psychological Treatments: A Review of Current Efforts," *American Psychologist*, Vol. 65, No. 2, 2010, pp. 73–84.

McIndoo, Crystal C., "Mindfulness-Based Therapy and Behavioral Activation: A Randomized Controlled Trial with Depressed College Students," *Behaviour Research and Therapy*, Vol. 77, 2016, pp. 118–128.

McManus, Freda, Sarah Rakovshik, Helen Kennerley, Melanie Fennell, and David Westbrook, "An Investigation of the Accuracy of Therapists' Self-Assessment of Cognitive-Behaviour Therapy Skills," *British Journal of Clinical Psychology*, Vol. 51, 2012, pp. 292–306.

Meier, Andrea, Mark P. McGovern, Chantal Lambert-Harris, Bethany McLeman, Anna Franklin, Elizabeth C. Saunders, and Haiyi Xie, "Adherence and Competence in Two Manual-Guided Therapies for Co-Occurring Substance Use and Posttraumatic Stress Disorders: Clinician Factors and Patient Outcomes," *American Journal of Drug and Alcohol Abuse*, Vol. 41, No. 6, 2015, pp. 527–534.

Miller, William R., Theresa B. Moyers, Lisa Arciniega, Denise Ernst, and Alyssa Forcehimes, "Training, Supervision and Quality Monitoring of the COMBINE Study Behavioral Interventions," *Journal of Studies on Alcohol Supplement*, Vol. 66, No. 15, 2005, pp. 188–195.

Monson, Candice M., Norman Shields, Michael K. Suvak, Jeanine E. M. Lane, Philippe Shnaider, Meredith S. H. Landy, Anne C. Wagner, Iris Sijercic, Tasoula Masina, Sonya G. Wanklyn, and Shannon Wiltsey Stirman, "A Randomized Controlled Effectiveness Trial of Training Strategies in Cognitive Processing Therapy for Posttraumatic Stress Disorder: Impact on Patient Outcomes," *Behavior Research and Therapy*, Vol. 110, 2018, pp. 31–40.

Morgenstern, Jon, Thomas J. Morgan, Barbara S. McCrady, Daniel S. Keller, and Kathleen M. Carroll, "Manual-Guided Cognitive-Behavioral Therapy Training: A Promising Method for Disseminating Empirically Supported Substance Abuse Treatments to the Practice Community," *Psychology of Addictive Behaviors*, Vol. 15, No. 2, 2001, pp. 83–88.

Papas, Rebecca K., John E. Sidle, Steve Martino, Joyce B. Baliddawa, Rogers Songole, Otieno E. Omolo, Benson N. Gakinya, Michael M. Mwaniki, Japheth O. Adina, Tobista Nafula, Willis D. Owino-Ong'or, Kendall J. Bryant, Kathleen M. Carroll, Joseph L. Goulet, Amy C. Justice, and Stephen A. Maisto, "Systematic Cultural Adaptation of Cognitive-Behavioral Therapy to Reduce Alcohol Use Among HIV-Infected Outpatients in Western Kenya," *AIDS and Behavior*, Vol. 14, No. 3, 2010, pp. 669–678.

Perepletchikova, Francheska, and Alan E. Kazdin, "Treatment Integrity and Therapeutic Change: Issues and Research Recommendations," *Clinical Psychology: Science and Practice*, Vol. 12, No. 4, 2005, pp. 365–383.

Puspitasari, Ajeng J., Jonathan W. Kanter, Andrew M. Busch, Rachel Leonard, Shira Dunsiger, Shawn Cahill, Christopher Martell, and Kelly Koerner, "A Randomized Controlled Trial of an Online, Modular, Active Learning Training Program for Behavioral Activation for Depression," *Journal of Consulting and Clinical Psychology*, Vol. 85, No. 8, 2017, pp. 814–825.

Puspitasari, Ajeng J., Jonathan W. Kanter, Joseph Murphy, Alex Crowe, and Kelly Koerner, "Developing an Online, Modular, Active Learning Training Program for Behavioral Activation," *Psychotherapy*, Vol. 50, No. 2, 2013, pp. 256–265.

Rakovshik, Sarah G., and Freda McManus, "Establishing Evidence-Based Training in Cognitive Behavioral Therapy: A Review of Current Empirical Findings and Theoretical Guidance," *Clinical Psychology Review*, Vol. 30, No. 5, 2010, pp. 496–516.

Rawson, Richard A., Solomon Rataemane, Lusanda Rataemane, Nomvuyo Ntlhe, Ruthlyn Sodano Fox, Jason McCuller, and Mary-Lynn Brecht, "Dissemination and Implementation of Cognitive Behavioral Therapy for Stimulant Dependence: A Randomized Trial Comparison of 3 Approaches," *Substance Abuse*, Vol. 34, No. 2, 2013, pp. 108–117.

Rhodes, Shelley, David A. Richards, David M. Ekers, Dean McMillan, Sarah Byford, Paul A. Farrand, Simon Gilbody, Steven D. Hollon, Willem Kuyken, Christopher Martell, Heather A. O'Mahen, Emer O'Neill, Nigel Reed, Rod S. Taylor, Ed R. Watkins, and Kim A. Wright, "Cost and Outcome of Behavioural Activation Versus Cognitive Behaviour Therapy for Depression (COBRA): Study Protocol for a Randomised Controlled Trial," *Trials*, Vol. 15, Article 29, 2014, pp. 1–12.

Rosen, Craig S., M. M. Matthieu, Shannon Wiltsey Stirman, J. M. Cook, S. Landes, N. C. Bernardy, K. M. Chard, J. Crowley, A. Eftekhari, E. P. Finley, J. L. Hamblen, J. M. Harik, S. M. Kehle-Forbes, L. A. Meis, P. E. Osei-Bonsu, A. L. Rodriguez, K. J. Ruggiero, J. I. Ruzek, B. N. Smith, L. Trent, and B. V. Watts, "A Review of Studies on the System-Wide Implementation of Evidence-Based Psychotherapies for Posttraumatic Stress Disorder in the Veterans Health Administration," *Administration and Policy in Mental Health and Mental Health Services Research*, Vol. 43, No. 6, 2016, pp. 957–977.

Rush, A. John, Mark Zimmerman, Stephen R. Wisniewski, Maurizio Fava, Steven D. Hollon, Diane Warden, Melanie M. Biggs, Kathy Shores-Wilson, Richard C. Shelton, James F. Luther, Brandi Thomas, and Madhukar H. Trivedi, "Comorbid Psychiatric Disorders in Depressed Outpatients: Demographic and Clinical Features," *Journal of Affective Disorders*, Vol. 87, No. 1, 2005, pp. 43–55.

Schoenwald, Sonja K., and Kimberly Hoagwood, "Effectiveness, Transportability, and Dissemination of Interventions: What Matters When?" *Psychiatric Services*, Vol. 52, No. 9, 2001, pp. 1190–1197.

Scott, Kelli, and Cara C. Lewis, "Using Measurement-Based Care to Enhance Any Treatment," *Cognitive and Behavioral Practice*, Vol. 22, No. 1, 2015, pp. 49–59.

Seal, Karen H., Greg Cohen, Angela Waldrop, Beth E. Cohen, Shira Maguen, and Li Ren, "Substance Use Disorders in Iraq and Afghanistan Veterans in VA Healthcare, 2001–2010: Implications for Screening, Diagnosis and Treatment," *Drug and Alcohol Dependence*, Vol. 116, Nos. 1–3, 2011, p. 93–101.

Shemesh, Eyal, Rachel A. Annunziato, Beth D. Weatherley, Gad Cotter, John R. Feaganes, Mugdha Santra, Rachel Yehuda, and David Rubinstein, "A Randomized Controlled Trial of the Safety and Promise of Cognitive-Behavioral Therapy Using Imaginal Exposure in Patients with Posttraumatic Stress Disorder Resulting from Cardiovascular Illness," *Journal of Clinical Psychiatry*, Vol. 72, No. 2, 2011, pp. 168–174.

Sholomskas, Diane E., and Kathleen M. Carroll, "One Small Step for Manuals: Computer-Assisted Training in Twelve-Step Facilitation," *Journal of Studies on Alcohol*, Vol. 67, No. 6, 2006, pp. 939–945.

Sholomskas, Diane E., Gia Syracuse-Siewert, Bruce J. Rounsaville, Samuel A. Ball, Kathryn F. Nuro, and Kathleen M. Carroll, "We Don't Train in Vain: A Dissemination Trial of Three Strategies of Training Clinicians in Cognitive-Behavioral Therapy," *Journal of Consulting and Clinical Psychology*, Vol. 73, No. 1, 2005, pp. 106–115.

Simons, Anne D., Christine A. Padesky, Jeremy Montemarano, Cara C. Lewis, Jessica Murakami, Kristen Lamb, Sharon DeVinney, Mark Reid, David A. Smith, and Aaron T. Beck, "Training and Dissemination of Cognitive Behavior Therapy for Depression in Adults: A Preliminary Examination of Therapist Competence and Client Outcomes," *Journal of Consulting and Clinical Psychology*, Vol. 78, No. 5, 2010, pp. 751–756.

Southam-Gerow, Michael A., Shannon E. Hourigan, and Robert B. Allin Jr., "Adapting Evidence-Based Mental Health Treatments in Community Settings: Preliminary Results from a Partnership Approach," *Behavior Modification*, Vol. 33, No. 1, 2009, pp. 82–103.

Stewart, Michael O., Susan D. Raffa, Jennifer L. Steele, Sarah A. Miller, Kathleen F. Clougherty, Gregory A. Hinrichsen, and Bradley E. Karlin, "National Dissemination of Interpersonal Psychotherapy for Depression in Veterans: Therapist and Patient-Level Outcomes," *Journal of Consulting and Clinical Psychology*, Vol. 82, No. 6, 2014, pp. 1201–1206.

Tanielian, Terri, Caroline Batka, and Lisa S. Meredith, *Bridging Gaps in Mental Health Care: Lessons Learned from the Welcome Back Veterans Initiative*, Santa Monica, Calif.: RAND Corporation, RR-2030-MTF, 2017. As of August 22, 2018:
https://www.rand.org/pubs/research_reports/RR2030.html

Tanielian, Terri, Coreen Farris, Caroline Batka, Carrie M. Farmer, Eric Robinson, Charles C. Engel, Michael Robbins, and Lisa H. Jaycox, *Ready to Serve: Community-Based Provider Capacity to Deliver Culturally Competent, Quality Mental Health Care to Veterans and Their Families*, Santa Monica, Calif.: RAND Corporation, RR-806-UNHF, 2014. As of August 22, 2018:
https://www.rand.org/pubs/research_reports/RR806.html

Tanielian, Terri, Lisa H. Jaycox, Terry L. Schell, Grant N. Marshall, M. Audrey Burnam, Christine Eibner, Benjamin Karney, Lisa S. Meredith, Jeanne S. Ringel, and Mary E. Vaiana, *Invisible Wounds: Summary and Recommendations for Addressing Psychological and Cognitive Injuries*, Santa Monica, Calif.: RAND Corporation, MG-720/1-CCF, 2008. As of August 22, 2018:
https://www.rand.org/pubs/monographs/MG720z1.html

U.S. Department of Veterans Affairs, "VA/DoD Clinical Practice Guidelines," 2018. As of July 16, 2018:
https://www.healthquality.va.gov/

Walser, Robyn D., Bradley E. Karlin, Mickey Trockel, Barbara Mazina, and C. Barr Taylor, "Training in and Implementation of Acceptance and Commitment Therapy for Depression in the Veterans Health Administration: Therapist and Patient Outcomes," *Behaviour Research and Therapy*, Vol. 51, No. 9, 2013, pp. 555–563.

Wang, Marilyn W., and Julian C. Stanley, "Differential Weighting: A Review of Methods and Empirical Studies," *Review of Educational Research*, Vol. 40, No. 5, 1970, pp. 663–705.

Watkins, Katherine E., Sarah B. Hunter, Suzanne L. Wenzel, Wenli Tu, Susan M. Paddock, Anne Griffin, and Patricia Ebener, "Prevalence and Characteristics of Clients with Co-Occurring Disorders in Outpatient Substance Abuse Treatment," *American Journal of Drug and Alcohol Abuse*, Vol. 30, No. 4, 2004, pp. 749–764.

Weck, Florian, Visar Rudari, Christine Hilling, Martin Hautzinger, Thomas Heidenreich, Karin Schermelleh-Engel, and Ulrich Stangier, "Relapses in Recurrent Depression 1 Year After Maintenance Cognitive-Behavioral Therapy: The Role of Therapist Adherence, Competence, and the Therapeutic Alliance," *Psychiatry Research*, Vol. 210, No. 1, 2013, pp. 140–145.

Wiltsey Stirman, Shannon, Cassidy A. Gutner, Kirsten Langdon, and Jessica R. Graham, "Bridging the Gap Between Research and Practice in Mental Health Service Settings: An Overview of Developments in Implementation Theory and Research," *Behavior Therapy*, Vol. 47, No. 6, 2016, pp. 920–936.

Wiltsey Stirman, Shannon, Kristin Pontoski, Torrey Creed, Regina Xhezo, Arthur C. Evans, Aaron T. Beck, and Paul Crits-Christoph, "A Non-Randomized Comparison of Strategies for Consultation in a Community-Academic Training Program to Implement an Evidence-Based Psychotherapy," *Administration and Policy in Mental Health and Mental Health Services Research*, Vol. 44, No. 1, 2017, pp. 55–66.